ALSO BY PHILLIP HOOSE

The Boys Who Challenged Hitler:
Knud Pedersen and the Churchill Club

Moonbird: A Year on the Wind with the Great Survivor B95

Claudette Colvin: Twice Toward Justice

Perfect, Once Removed: When Baseball Was All the World to Me

We Were There, Too!: Young People in U.S. History

Hey, Little Ant (with Hannah Hoose)

It's Our World, Too!: Young People Who Are Making a Difference—
How They Do It, and How You Can, Too!

Necessities: Racial Barriers in American Sports

Hoosiers: The Fabulous Basketball Life of Indiana

Building an Ark: Tools for the Preservation of
Natural Diversity Through Land Protection

ATTUCKS!

PHILLIP HOOSE

Oscar Robertson and the Basketball Team That Awakened a City

Farrar Straus Giroux
New York

Farrar Straus Giroux Books for Young Readers
An imprint of Macmillan Publishing Group, LLC
175 Fifth Avenue, New York, NY 10010

fiercereads.com

Library of Congress Cataloging-in-Publication Data

Names: Hoose, Phillip M., 1947– author.
Title: Attucks! : Oscar Robertson and the basketball team that awakened a city / Phillip Hoose.
Description: First edition. | New York : Farrar Straus Giroux Books for Young Readers, 2018. |
    Includes bibliographical references and index.
Identifiers: LCCN 2018002809 | ISBN 9780374306120 (hardcover)
Subjects: LCSH: Crispus Attucks Tigers (Basketball team)—History. | Robertson, Oscar, 1938– |
    Basketball players—United States—Biography.
Classification: LCC GV885.43.C8 H66 2018 | DDC 796.323092 [B] —dc23
LC record available at https://lccn.loc.gov/2018002809

Our books may be purchased in bulk for promotional, educational,
or business use. Please contact your local bookseller or the Macmillan
Corporate and Premium Sales Department at (800) 221-7945 ext. 5442
or by email at MacmillanSpecialMarkets@macmillan.com.

**Frontispiece: As good as it got: Oscar Robertson launches a one-hander
in a tournament game at Butler Fieldhouse.**
(Indiana Basketball Hall of Fame)

For Wilma Moore and Dr. Stanley Warren,
historians and teachers who have lived this story and kept it alive

Contents

ATTUCKS!

A Note from the Author
Oscar's Contention

Whites could see his talent; but what whites did not know was the special niche Oscar Robertson had in the hearts of black athletes everywhere. For it was Oscar, as a player at an all-black school in Indianapolis called Crispus Attucks, who had led his team to the state championship in 1955 and 1956. The state tourney in Indiana was something of a national event, and until then it had been a white-dominated event . . . There were thousands and thousands of blacks who had never set foot inside Indiana who knew what had happened.

—David Halberstam, *The Breaks of the Game*

I grew up in Speedway, Indiana, a community connected by a bridge to Indianapolis. On the east side of the Sixteenth Street Bridge, it was—and is—Indianapolis; on the west, it was Speedway. When I moved there with my family in 1956, Speedway had eleven thousand residents, all of whom were white except for one family—the Burtons. Evelyn, the family's only child, was in my fourth-grade class. She was tall and slender, had a high-pitched laugh, and liked to jump rope on the playground. I never worked up the nerve to speak to her, though I was endlessly curious about her. How did she come to be with us? Did it feel any different to have dark skin like hers rather than light skin like mine? What would it be like to talk with her? What did she think of us?

There were even greater mysteries on the Indianapolis side of the bridge. Somewhere in Indianapolis there was said to be "a school where all black kids in the city went." The name sounded strange: Crispus Attucks (pronounced "Áttix"). We all called it "Christmas"

Attucks, not to make fun but because that's what we thought the name was. No one in Speedway seemed to have any idea where this school was. It was just out there somewhere, south of Sixteenth Street by the baseball stadium, they said, and not that far away.

On Saturdays, my dad sometimes drove us into Indianapolis to shop at the downtown department stores. As we approached the White River and the central part of the city, we passed through a neighborhood of slumping, ramshackle frame houses, most bigger than ours but more run-down. Kids ran around in the front yards, just like my friends and I did in Speedway. But they all had dark skin. Gazing out the car window, I wondered the same kinds of things about those kids as I wondered about Evelyn: Did they play what I played? Did they have TVs? Did they watch my shows? Were they happy? What would happen if I jumped out of the car and ran over to try to play with them? Why was everyone in this neighborhood black whereas almost everyone in my town was white?

The only actual contact we in Speedway had with African Americans was through the Indiana High School Basketball Tournament. Sometimes Speedway was in the same sectional round as Attucks, and we occasionally played against them. We never beat them, though. In Speedway, the Attucks team was legendary. Attucks had won the entire state tournament—beating out more than seven hundred other teams—the year before my family arrived in Speedway. Their star player, Oscar Robertson, was said to be the greatest basketball player ever in Indiana. People talked about him all the time; he was probably the most famous person in the city. Oscar had such an impact that three years after he graduated from high school and left Indianapolis to live in Cincinnati, a newspaper poll still proclaimed Oscar Robertson to be the most admired person in Indianapolis.

In 1986, long after I had left Indiana to move east, I had a chance to meet Oscar Robertson and have a long talk with him. *Sports Illustrated* magazine hired me to go to Indiana to conduct interviews for a story on what made Indiana basketball-crazy. I talked with dozens and dozens of coaches and players, historians and newspaper columnists, cheerleaders and fans. But there was one interview I wanted above all others: Oscar Robertson, the famed "Big O," who had achieved greatness as a college and NBA player. Oscar agreed to sit down with me in his lawyer's office in Cincinnati. We talked for a full three hours, mostly about what it had been like going to Crispus Attucks High School in Indianapolis, that mysterious school that had aroused my curiosity when I was young.

One scrap from that conversation inspired the book you're reading now.

"You know," Oscar said, "when the Ku Klux Klan started our school, they really didn't understand what they were doing."

"What do you mean?" I asked.

"They did something they couldn't foresee by making Attucks an all-black school. The city of Indianapolis integrated because we were winning. All the black guys, the really great players, went to Attucks. We were winning all those games, and the coaches didn't like it. And then a lot of black kids started going to other schools . . ."

What could he be talking about? A high school in a major American city—in the North—started by the Ku Klux Klan? And a basketball team integrating that city?

Oscar wasn't laughing.

Could it be true?

Looking back on the civil rights movement, Dr. Martin Luther King Jr. observed, "The blanket of fear was lifted by the Negro youth of the nation." There are many examples of young people who had sacrificed in various ways for racial justice. In 1951, a Farmville, Virginia, high school junior named Barbara Johns led her classmates out of their all-black school to protest their overcrowded building, broken-down desks, and inferior supplies. In March 1955—almost a year before Rosa Parks famously did the same thing—Claudette Colvin, a fifteen-year-old Montgomery, Alabama, ninth grader, refused to surrender her public bus seat to a white passenger and then found the courage to challenge the bus segregation laws in court. Two years later, nine students guarded by federal troops became the first African Americans to attend Central High School in Little Rock, Arkansas. The list goes on and on.

But not all the change-making events took place in southern states, and not all involved clashes, water cannons, troops, courtrooms, or attack dogs.

And when I looked into it, I discovered that, as Oscar Robertson had suggested during our conversation, the rise of a schoolboy basketball team was the most memorable civil rights episode in the history of one major American city. Just how much did Crispus Attucks High's mighty surge mean to blacks—and many whites—in Indianapolis? The morning after Attucks's greatest victory, the *Indianapolis Recorder*, a weekly newspaper serving the city's African American readers, did its best to explain:

Persons unfamiliar with our state may believe that we are overdoing it in going down on our knees and giving praise to Almighty

God that this glorious thing has come to pass. But basketball—especially the high school variety—occupies a particularly lofty place in the Hoosier scheme of things. It is far more than a boys' sport—in fact, it is just about the most important thing there is.

Prologue

Flap's Shot

"The Fence" was a tired old play, used to score the last basket at the end of a close game. The team's tallest player took the ball out of bounds under his team's basket while his four teammates stood shoulder to shoulder at the free-throw line, forming a wall in front of the opposing players guarding them. The tall passer looped the ball over the human wall to the team's best shooter, who stepped back from the fence formation to receive the pass and take the last shot. It was one of the oldest plays in basketball. Everyone knew it. Including Anderson High.

But that was the play Crispus Attucks's coach, Ray Crowe, had drawn up with Attucks possessing the ball and behind by one point, 80—79, with seven seconds left. The play was designed for the team's best shooter, Hallie Bryant, to step back from the fence and take the crucial shot.

The referee handed the ball to Attucks center Bob Jewell, who stood out of bounds beneath Attucks's basket, holding the ball with two hands above his head. The ref blew his whistle to begin the most important seven seconds in the history of basketball in Indianapolis.

The play was a disaster from the first tick. Anderson had it deciphered perfectly, guarding Hallie Bryant too tightly for Jewell to reach him with a pass. Bailey Robertson, a reserve guard whom everyone called "Flap," was the first to sense disaster. With no time to lose, he broke from the fence, sprinted to the right corner, and turned to face Jewell. Jewell, out of options, whipped the ball across his body to Flap Robertson, who caught it, squared his body to support the shot, aimed, jumped as high as he could, and launched the ball with his right hand.

Bailey "Flap" Robertson shooting at Lockefield Gardens in the Dust Bowl Tournament. (Indiana Basketball Hall of Fame)

ATTUCKS WINS

Indi
IN

Fifty-sixth Year

Coach Spurlock "Never" Gave U Hope of Victory

Alber¹ C. Spurlock, assista
coach of the net-cutting Tiger
hadn't given the game up for lo
when Attucks was 10 points be
hind with only four and a ha
minutes left to play. But he ha
given up when Jack Tilley sa
his second free throw to put A
derson out front 80 to 79, with 2
seconds to go.

As a matter of fact, when ⁵
Tigers brought the ball in fro
under the Anderson basket ar
started the seconds to ticking of
Spurlock said he and Coach Ra

The headline says it all: Flap Robertson's shot shocked the city, put Attucks on the map, and touched off a celebration in Frog Island.
(*Indianapolis Recorder*)

Twenty-four years of community struggle rested on the shot as it spun tightly above the Butler Fieldhouse floor. A quarter century's progress hung in the balance as Flap's wrist remained frozen in a classic shooter's follow-through. The now-descending shot, if it fell through the hoop, would answer those who had built a school to fail in a hateful atmosphere, would speak to those who kept Attucks High from playing in the tournament for fifteen long years, would reply to those who felt that black athletes would wilt under pressure. Flap Robertson's shot was a once-in-a-lifetime, all-or-nothing bid for respect.

As with many legendary events, the details of what happened next are open to debate. Oscar Robertson, Flap's then-twelve-year-old brother—who, a decade later, would be known throughout America as "the Big O"—was watching the 1951 Indianapolis regional championship game at home on TV with his mom and brother Henry. Thirty-five years later, he remembered Flap's shot as a "Hail Mary," one that

"struck the rim, bounced up, and fell straight down through the net." Hallie Bryant, the Fence play's intended receiver, recalled that the ball rattled around the hoop before dropping through, almost of fatigue. But for the rest of his life, Flap Robertson would have none of that.

"Nothin' but net," he recalled years later to an interviewer, nodding vigorously. "People told me their relatives died of heart attacks. One lady said she started to go into labor when the ball went through. And ever since, I've asked myself, 'Why me?' Well, there's no answer. I wasn't even on the starting team. I guess that fate just said, 'Go in, Flap.'"

Fate's broad smile that day reached Flap's youngest brother as well. "After Flap's shot," Oscar Robertson later wrote, "things would never be the same again for me. I knew it. For the first time, a candle of hope flickered inside my heart."

A Florida family packed and ready to head north. (Library of Congress)

North Toward Hope

From Florida's stormy banks I go;
I've bid the South "Good by";
No longer shall they treat me so,
And knock me in the eye.

—Mr. Ward, "Bound for the Promised Land,"
originally published in the *Chicago Defender*, November 11, 1916

Most of the boys who played on Indianapolis's Crispus Attucks High School teams of the 1950s were born in the South. At some point, adults in their lives led them aboard buses or trains and ushered them to the rear. The buses coughed to life and pulled out of the stations, swinging into a long journey toward hope. Children waved tearful goodbyes to grandparents and cousins and aunts and uncles until everyone disappeared from sight. After an hour or so, the adults pulled chicken and pound cake out of grease-stained brown-paper bags and passed the food around. Crying stopped.

They traveled on odd-numbered two-lane highways—31 and 41

and 51 and 61—bound north toward an auntie's house or an uncle's garage in the city called Indianapolis. Children pressed their noses against smudged windows, gazing at barns and cows whizzing by; at sleek, shiny horses prancing behind white fences in Kentucky; at signs that said SEE MAMMOTH CAVE. Years later, the players could still recite the names of the towns they had passed through as children: Jackson, Hendersonville, Millersville, Bowling Green, Paducah, Horse Cave, Elizabethtown, Henderson. They watched the strings of little white roadside signs that made an advertising jingle a few words at a time: PAST / SCHOOLHOUSES / TAKE IT SLOW / LET THE LITTLE / SHAVERS GROW / BURMA-SHAVE. Billboards for Mammoth Cave grew bigger and more frequent, then disappeared when the road to Kentucky's famed underground attraction slid away.

When the bus stopped, which it did every hour or so, the passengers filed out and went around to the back of the gas station or other building to the "colored" bathrooms and water fountains, where they stood around until they heard the driver holler to get back on. When they crossed the Ohio River on the Second Street Bridge, passing from Louisville, Kentucky, to Jeffersonville, Indiana—the North—most of the future basketball stars were sound asleep, perhaps dreaming of the flat brown fields they had worked and played in with friends they might never see again.

One such family came north from Bellsburg, Tennessee. In the winter of 1942, Mazell Robertson and her three sons—Bailey, nine; Henry, six; and Oscar, four—boarded a Greyhound bus in Nashville, Tennessee, bound for Indianapolis, a city with about four hundred thousand inhabitants. Hearts were heavy. They were leaving their extended family and the three hundred acres of cornfields that Mazell's grandfather, still alive at 112, had begun to sharecrop not long after the Civil War. Mazell's husband, Bailey Sr., had gone to

Indianapolis some months before, looking for factory work. The factory jobs had been held by whites, but now many of them had gone overseas to fight. With the armed forces largely segregated, Bailey Robertson Sr. had hoped to find a good-paying job in a defense plant, but when nothing turned up, he had signed on with the city sanitation department. It wasn't much, but it was steady. The family should come on up now, he said. They could all stay with his sister Inez until they could find a place of their own.

To Mazell Robertson, there was no choice but to leave. All black children from first through sixth grade in Dickson County, Tennessee, took their lessons in a one-room schoolhouse, led by a single saintly teacher named Lizzie Gleves. Little boys and girls who were barely toilet-trained sat down beside older children who were already seasoned farmhands. Boys were constantly pulled out of class to help with farm work, and they were glad to go. Mazell Robertson asked herself, "How much could my boys learn in that room?" Whatever Indianapolis was, it had to be more than this. Whatever Indianapolis was, it was the North.

At the end of the eight-hour journey, sometime after midnight, the bus pulled into the Illinois Street Greyhound station in Indianapolis. The Robertsons dragged their only suitcase, bound together with baling wire, off the bus and into the terminal. For some reason, Aunt Inez was not there to meet them. They waited for a couple of hours, then got restless. They had no experience with Indianapolis's trolleys or city buses, but they knew very well how to walk long distances. Together they pushed and pulled and kneed the suitcase sixteen blocks along Senate Avenue toward the address on Mazell's scrap of paper.

As Bailey remembered it years later, the house was dark and the door locked. They huddled together on the porch until morning, when Inez came home from work and let them in. She said she hadn't known they were coming.

They would stay with Aunt Inez for another year, until Bailey Sr. could finally put a deposit on a house nearby.

Bailey, Henry, and Oscar Robertson, like most of the other future Crispus Attucks High School basketball players, were part of the Great Migration, the exodus of fed-up blacks who poured out of the South and funneled into northern cities as if the map itself had tilted north. Hopeful black families surged into New York, Chicago, Cleveland, and Detroit. Another destination was Indianapolis, Indiana, popular in part because it was so close to the South, where beloved family members remained.

The Great Migration

Between 1916 and 1970, nearly six million African Americans migrated north to seek jobs, better housing, and a good education for children. North also meant hope, hope for relief from white people who hated and threatened and confined and belittled them, exploiting their labor for a fraction of its worth.

The southern boys who as teenagers in the 1950s would revolutionize the game of basketball came to "Naptown," as Indianapolis was often called, on two-lane highways when they were children in the 1930s and '40s. The adults in their lives had plans and dreams, and had staked everything on a better chance in a big northern city.

The boys who were converging on Indianapolis would wield an enormous impact on their future home, though they had no way of knowing it. Willie Gardner, whose powerhouse dunks would amaze some and disgust others, came north on a bus with his mom from Pulaski, Tennessee. Hallie Bryant, pioneer of the one-handed jump shot, motored north from South Carolina with his dad in 1942. Hook-shooting Sheddrick Mitchell journeyed all the way from Mississippi, while high-flying Willie Merriweather rode north from Tennessee with his dad in the old man's Buick convertible. Father

14

and son both loved to feel the power of the stylish automobile. When he got pulled over for speeding, Willie's dad would slap on a chauffeur's hat and tell the officer he was delivering the car to a white man.

And also from Tennessee came Mazell Robertson's boys. The eldest, Bailey, would deliver Attucks High to national prominence on the wings of his buzzer-beating shot from the corner in 1951. Middle son Henry would become a valuable reserve on a great Attucks team. And youngest brother Oscar, a dozen years from being acclaimed the most brilliant high school player ever from Indiana, would leave his mark on everything.

Black families arriving were shocked by the Indianapolis that greeted them. Jim Crow's wings shadowed everything. Schools were racially segregated, just as in the South. Most black families lived in overcrowded squalor within a damp, low-lying slum neighborhood known as Frog Island. Most houses had no heat, electricity, or indoor plumbing.

Many black women worked as maids, taking their meals on the back porches of the houses they cleaned, raising the children of rich whites for a few dollars a day. Signs announced parks as WHITE or COLORED. Blacks were universally unwelcome. City Hospital treated black patients in only one ward.

Jim Crow

Throughout the United States, and particularly in the South, the races were segregated by a densely woven web of laws, signs, partitions, arrows, ordinances, unequal opportunities, rules, insults, threats, and customs—often backed up by violence. Together, the whole system of racial segregation was known as "Jim Crow," its informal name taken from an 1830s vaudeville character that depicted blacks negatively.

Frog Island, the neglected Indianapolis slum into which most of the city's African Americans were crowded. (O. James Fox Collection, Indiana Historical Society)

Blacks were shunned in downtown department stores and banished to the balconies of movie theaters. Even the city's Riverside Amusement Park accepted black children only on "Colored Frolic Day," which came once a year *if* your family had amassed enough milk-bottle caps from the local dairy. Signs throughout the park said WHITE PATRONAGE ONLY SOLICITED. "But isn't Indiana supposed to be in the *North*?" the new arrivals asked one another. How could a northern city feel as hostile as the places they had just come from?

Indiana had never been welcoming to blacks. One 1831 law, renewed in 1851 by widespread popular vote, required blacks entering Indiana to "register" for residency. That meant they had to present themselves at their local county courthouse with a witness and post a $500 bond. Registration was supposed to guarantee that blacks desiring to live in Indiana would not become "beggars or criminals."

But during the Great Migration, nothing could stop the tide of hopeful black families who continued to exit the South and pour northward across the Ohio River, some settling in small towns just on the Indiana side of the river, but more pushing on northward to the state capital, Indianapolis. By 1920, around thirty-five thousand African Americans lived in Indianapolis, more than twice the number who had lived there twenty years earlier. Many whites viewed the migration as an invasion—one that had to be stopped.

Enter David Curtis Stephenson. In 1921, this twenty-nine-year-old coal company salesman was hired by Ku Klux Klan recruiter Joseph Huffington to build a Klavern—a Klan chapter—in Evansville, Indiana. Stephenson was a stocky, handsome, tastefully dressed man with a full head of blond hair and a ready smile. No one seemed to know much about him; really, there wasn't much to know. He had quit school in the eighth grade and drifted around the Great

D. C. Stephenson, Grand Dragon of the Indiana Ku Klux Klan. "I am the law in Indiana," Stephenson often proclaimed, and in the early 1920s, it was close to the truth. (Indiana Historical Society)

Plains, making his living as a typesetter in print shops. He married early and deserted his pregnant wife.

Steve, as he liked to be called, was a spellbinding storyteller who mesmerized lawyers, bankers, and farmers alike. He drank heavily and had an eager eye for women. He also had a genius for organization. Stephenson sized up Indiana and saw in an instant how the Klan could make him a king. In 1920, Indiana had the highest percentage of native-born white residents of any state in the Union. That meant that many Indiana residents had not traveled widely and were suspicious of outsiders.

Stephenson gave them enemies to fear and hate. In fiery speeches, Stephenson condemned Catholics, blacks, and Jews as "aliens" who had invaded Indiana to control money, steal jobs, and attack white women.

A pamphlet entitled "Ideals of the Klan" described the Klan as follows:

- This is a white man's organization.
- This is a Gentile organization.
- It is an American organization.
- It is a Protestant organization.

Thousands flocked to hear Stephenson speak at Klan "Field Days." One 1923 speech in Kokomo's Malfalfa Park attracted two hundred thousand people, one of the biggest public gatherings in the history of Indiana. Stephenson arrived late by private plane. When the propellers slowed to a halt, the door popped open and there he was, dusting off his suit, sweeping back his blond hair, squinting at the sun. He began his speech by apologizing for his tardiness, explaining, "The president of the United States kept me unduly long counseling upon vital matters of state." When the cheering died, Stephenson lit into what he called the forces of evil: Our country is being stolen from us by outsiders. It's time for "One Hundred Percent Americans" to wake up and take Indiana back! Similar rhetoric would propel Adolf Hitler to power in just a few years.

By 1924, nearly one-third of Indiana's white male population—about 250,000 in all—were Klan members, and Indiana was known far and wide as the Klan State. Historian Irving Leibowitz later wrote, "In the rural counties, from the gently undulating prairies of northeastern Indiana to the impoverished hill farms of southern Indiana, more than half the citizens were members of the Klan . . . Nearly 500,000 Hoosiers, in white robes and hoods, burned their fiery

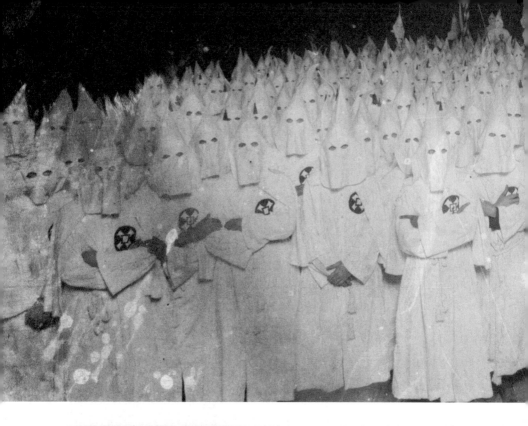

(Top) A nighttime Muncie, Indiana, Ku Klux Klan rally, sixty miles northeast of Indianapolis, in 1922, a time when nearly one of every three white males was a Klansman. (Bottom left) Citizens of Marion, Indiana, kneel in prayer at a Klan rally, with burning cross visible behind altar. (Bottom right) Four Muncie Camelias, as "auxiliary" female Klan members were known, are shown without their veils in 1924. (Ball State University, Archives and Special Collections)

crosses almost nightly to strike fear in the hearts of their neighbors." Stephenson quickly became a millionaire by marketing what one writer later called "a hysteria of belonging." He dressed like a banker, in tailored suits, and traveled with bodyguards. Tens of thousands of white Protestant Hoosiers bought Klan memberships for between $10 and $25, of which Stephenson pocketed $4. White robes and peaked hats went for $6 a set, of which Stephenson kept $4.25.

Within eighteen months, D. C. Stephenson had raked in more than $2 million—by peddling fear. In 1923, he had been appointed Grand Dragon (state leader) of the Ku Klux Klan in Indiana and head of recruiting for seven other states. "I'm a nobody from nowhere, really," Stephenson liked to say. "But I've got the brains. I'm going to be the biggest man in the United States."

Overnight, common people—responsible parents, good neighbors, community leaders—pulled hoods over their heads and fanned out in mobs under the cover of darkness to terrorize the homes and workplaces of blacks, Jews, and Catholics. Crosses soaked in kerosene blazed on hillsides. Billboards reading NIGGER, DON'T LET THE SUN SET ON YOU HERE cast long shadows at many Indiana town lines.

On primary election day in 1922, the Klan ran a motorcade through Frog Island, firing revolvers into the air to pin citizens indoors so they wouldn't go out to vote. In 1924, Ed Jackson, a Republican who had campaigned from the backseat of Stephenson's Cadillac, was elected governor of Indiana by a landslide. The voters also swept in dozens of Klan-friendly legislators, prosecutors, judges, mayors, and local community leaders throughout Indiana.

Shortly after the 1924 elections, Stephenson sat back in his grand mansion in the Irvington neighborhood of Indianapolis and summed up all he had accomplished with a single sentence: "I am the law in Indiana," he crowed.

It was all too true.

• • •

In the early 1920s, the Klan-influenced Indianapolis school board turned its attention to public education. For decades, black and white students had studied together in the city's elementary, junior high, and high schools. It hadn't been perfect—black students often sat clumped together at the back of the classroom, and team sports and club activities were segregated. But to a degree it worked, and black students were able to get a decent education in the city's public schools.

At the height of the Klan years, there were eight hundred African American high school students attending the city's four high schools. White neighborhood groups howled for segregated schools. The Indianapolis Chamber of Commerce petitioned the school board in 1922 for funds to build a "separate, modern, completely equipped, and adequate high school building for colored students." Blacks contracted tuberculosis more frequently than whites, some people claimed, so a separate school was needed to quarantine black students and head off a public health crisis.

That December, the school board, citing the "laudable desire of Negroes for a high school education," recommended construction of a new blacks-only high school that would encourage "self-reliance," "initiative," and "good citizenship."

The vote was unanimous, 4—0. Most black parents objected. They understood that the *real* point of an all-black school was to separate students and their teachers by race. It was a hateful, isolating act.

In July 1924, the school board paid $3,400 for a lot facing Twelfth Street near West Street as the site for the proposed school. Black leaders sued to stop construction, but it was no use. The legal actions were only able to stop the school board from naming the new high school Thomas Jefferson High. Community leaders named it

The *Recorder*'s front-page coverage of the opening of Crispus Attucks is surrounded by evidence of the discrimination and violence faced by the city's African American community. (*Indianapolis Recorder*)

ATTUCKS HIGH WILL OPEN SEPT. 12TH

Building Fully Equipped Enrollment of 1200 Expected

By J. Ernest Webb

The Crispus Attucks High School will open for work, September 12, in keeping with the organization of the schools of the city. According to the records from the other high schools, it is thought that it will open with approximately 1200 students. The school authorities are to be congratulated on the type of the faculty selected. Practically all of the large colleges and universities are represented and outstanding results are expected from the teaching force.

We feel certain that our boys and girls will be well taken care of from the point of view of instruction.

The building has been wonderfully equipped by the Board, meeting the standard of the school system. A few of the outstanding features of the building are the Auditorium, Cafeteral, Music Department, Library, Science Laboratories and Commercial Department. Much could be said of all of the above, but we shall only speak of one or two.

The Auditorium has a seating capacity of approximately 875 with a gymnasium and stage so arranged that spectators may sit in the Auditorium and watch basket ball games in the gymnasium. The decoration and lighting facilities of the Auditorium are unsurpassed in

(Continued on page 2)

(Continued from page 1)

the city.

The Cafeteria will operate in three shifts being able to serve 350 at each shift.

The parents of children attending Crispus Attucks High School, will be delighted with the fact that the Board of School Commissioners have purchased many beautiful musical instruments for the boys and girls of the High School making it possibel to have a band and an orchestra. It has generally been understood that Attucks High School will be made a musical center and we are certain that the people of the city will not be disappointed. Provisions will be made for all lines of musical development, both instrumental and vocal.

It has been the delight of the boys who are to enter the high school to learn that provisions have been made to offer Military Training to all who wish to take it. Major Cathro, who has charge of the R. O. T. C. work of the city has arranged with Mr. Nolcox, Principal of Crispus Attucks High School, for a definite line of work including target practice and all details connected with his line of work.

Many inquiries from time to time have been made relative to what will be offered in the Program of Studies for the high school. On making inquiry of the principal, Mr. Nolcox, it was stated that all subjects signed up for in sufficient numbers would be offered including Spanish, French, Latin, Commercial Studies, Industrial Work, and etc., found in the other high schools of the ctiy. When Mr. Nolcox was asked about the ranking of the colored high school, he answered, "We are not planning a colored high school, but we are planning a high school and this high school must meet the standards from every point of view."

themselves after Crispus Attucks, a black seaman who was killed by British soldiers in the lead-up to the Revolutionary War.

Crispus Attucks: First to Defy, First to Die

An 1850s portrait of the Boston Massacre by William L. Champney features the mortally wounded Crispus Attucks in the center. (Boston Athenæum)

In 1770, Crispus Attucks was the first man to die in what became known as the Boston Massacre—an encounter between a group of American protesters and British soldiers that became a rallying cry used by patriots such as Paul Revere to encourage rebellion against the British authorities. Attucks's father was believed to be from Africa, and his mother was a Native American. As a slave boy, Attucks acquired skill in buying and selling cattle on the Framingham, Massachusetts, farm where he lived.

At the age of twenty-seven, Attucks escaped enslavement. Over the next twenty years he worked as a sailor on a whaling crew and as a ropemaker in Boston. He was in Boston as tensions between the British colonial government and American revolutionaries intensified. A fight between Boston ropemakers and three British soldiers erupted on Friday, March 2, 1770, setting the stage for a second round the following Monday night. Then a group of about thirty tradesmen taunted a British guard at the customhouse, hurling snowballs, sticks, and insults. Seven other redcoats rushed to the guard's rescue and opened fire. Crispus Attucks was one of five men killed—although later in court the soldiers (defended by future American president John Adams) were acquitted of the charge of murder, with Attucks portrayed as having initiated the fight, "with one hand [taking] hold of a bayonet, and with the other [knocking] the man down."

Initially regarded by some as members of "a motley rabble," Attucks and the other victims became symbols of the fight for liberty. Citizens of Boston observed the anniversary of the Boston Massacre in the years leading up to the Revolutionary War. Crispus Attucks's legend as a black hero grew. He became known as "the first to defy, the first to die."

On the morning of September 12, 1927, the doors to Indianapolis's Crispus Attucks High School swung open. A three-story redbrick building set in the northwest corner of Frog Island, it was too small from day one. A total of 1,385 students, many of them children from other neighborhoods uprooted from their local schools, squeezed through the columned arches at the school's front door and made their way toward their classrooms. It was nearly double the turnout expected by city school officials.

Across the state, the Klan's influence had faded a bit by 1927, largely because D. C. Stephenson had two years earlier been convicted of kidnapping, raping, mutilating, and murdering his secretary, an Indianapolis woman named Madge Oberholtzer. "Ed Jackson'll pardon me," Stephenson said, grinning, as they led him away. Twenty-five years later another governor did grant Stephenson parole, on the condition that the sun never set on him again in Indiana.

But there were still enough Klansmen around for a show of muscle on the first day of school at Attucks. In a history of the school, the *Indianapolis Star* wrote years later that "parades of masked Klansmen were organized. One parade on Washington Street, consisting

Crispus Attucks High School just after it opened in 1927. Though it was underfunded and overcrowded, it was excellent from the first day. (Bass Photo Co. Collection, Indiana Historical Society)

of row after row of masked Klansmen marching slowly to the beat of muffled drums, took an hour to pass."

It was in this atmosphere that the black children of Indianapolis opened their books in their new home.

Fifteen years later, in 1942, Mazell Robertson, with Bailey Jr., Henry, and Oscar, fresh from Tennessee, turned up on Aunt Inez's porch to start their lives anew in a northern city. When daylight arrived, they would discover that they had landed in a slum in a city widely known as "the South of the North."

The Robertsons did not yet know the rules that governed life on Indianapolis's near West Side, nor were they aware of all the hateful groundwork that the Klan-influenced politicians had laid a generation before to make black residents feel rejected and inferior. Neither did they know of a school called Crispus Attucks, or of the school's basketball coach Ray Crowe, or of the historic contribution to Indiana these brothers would make through a game called basketball.

They didn't know it yet, but their day was coming.

KING ARTHUR TRESTER

Arthur Trester, autocratic ruler of the ISHAA in its glory days. For fifteen years, "King Arthur" refused to allow black and parochial schools to play in the Indiana High School Basketball Tournament. (Courtesy Dale Glenn)

Hoosier Hysteria

"Round my Indiana Homestead" (as they sang in years gone by)
Now the basketballs are flying and they almost hide the sky;
For each gym is full of players and each town is full of gyms
As a hundred thousand snipers shoot their goals with deadly glims.
Old New York may have its subway with its famous Rum Row trust
And old Finland with its Nurm runs our runners into dust
But where candlelights are gleaming through the sycamores afar
Every son of Indiana shoots his basket like a star.

—Grantland Rice, "Back in 1925"

In the late summer of 1927, a few days after Indianapolis's Crispus Attucks High opened its doors to its first students, a trio of respected black leaders admiringly known as "the Big Three"—F. E. DeFranz, Reverend H. L. Herod, and F. B. Ransom—motored to Anderson, Indiana, to apply in person for Attucks's membership in the Indiana High School Athletic Association (IHSAA).

The IHSAA governed high school sports in Indiana. Membership would give Attucks High the chance to compete in sports events against the other schools of the state. Importantly, it would give Attucks the chance to play in Indiana's nationally famous high school basketball tournament—the biggest hoops show on earth. That would let everyone know that Attucks's athletes, regardless of the color of their skin, belonged to Indiana's family of schools.

The Big Three were shown into the office of the IHSAA's permanent secretary, Arthur Trester. Now in his eleventh year on the job, Trester had ridden the Indiana High School Basketball Tournament to fame and almost dictatorial power. He was widely known as "King Arthur" and "the Czar of the IHSAA." One newspaper caricatured him sitting on a globe and wearing a top hat with his arms crossed. That seemed about right. Square-shouldered, jut-jawed, and bulky, he signaled blunt authority.

More than any other individual, Arthur Trester had made Indiana America's basketball crossroads. The game had been invented in a Massachusetts YMCA in 1891. Its originator, physical education teacher James Naismith, saw basketball as something that city kids could do indoors in winter. Two years later, the game reached Indiana and proved just as good a fit for Hoosier farm boys. Basketball gave them something to do between fall harvesting and spring planting of crops. Most Indiana towns were too small in those years to produce football teams, and too poor to buy the pads and helmets anyway. But basketball required only five players on a team and very little equipment. Players could practice on their own simply by nailing a hoop to a barn or a woodshed. The game could be played indoors or outside.

What Is a Hoosier?

Unfortunately, the exact meaning of the word "Hoosier," used for a resident of Indiana, is lost to the ages. Through the years, the word has come to mean "friendly," "rural," "rugged," and "untamed."

James Whitcomb Riley, canonized as "the Hoosier Poet," gave a popular definition: "The early settlers were vicious fighters, and they not only gouged and scratched, but frequently bit off noses and ears. A settler coming into a barroom after a fight, and seeing an ear on the floor, would merely push it aside with his foot and carelessly ask, 'Whose ear?'"

For basketball purposes, poet John Bartlow Martin wrote: "Hoosiers say, 'First you put two peach baskets on posts; then you build your high school around them.'"

Indiana's state high school basketball tournament began in 1911 when thirteen teams—one from each Hoosier congressional district—were invited to compete in a single-elimination tournament at the Bloomington campus of Indiana University (IU). The winner would be crowned state champion. The event was for boys only, even though some Indiana schools already had girls' teams. (It would take another sixty-five years and an act of Congress for girls to get a tourney of their own in Indiana.)

Fans packed the IU fieldhouse for the first tournament. Even more came the next year. The third year's event showcased Indiana's first basketball superstar, a lanky farm boy named Homer Stonebraker who had learned to shoot by flinging a small rubber ball through a hoop nailed to his barn. "Stoney," as everyone called him, had no idea how good he had become, but by the time he was old enough for Wingate High, Stoney could shoot accurately from almost anyplace on a basketball floor. In the second game of the season, he shocked basketball fans throughout Indiana by scoring 80 points all by himself. Fevered curiosity about "Stoney and the Gymless Wonders" swept through the state and attracted mobs to Bloomington in March. Stoney turned out to be even better than advertised. Wingate won both the 1913 and 1914 state championship tournaments. In one quarterfinal game, Stoney scored every one of his team's points.

"Hoosier Hysteria" was born. In the next decade alone, tournament entries increased from 13 schools to 394. Communities built gyms that seated several times the school's enrollment—sometimes even more than the town's entire population—not only to accommodate all the basketball fans from outlying areas who lived for Friday night, but also to seize the home-court advantage in the first, or "sectional," round of the tourney.

Gym wars erupted. Little towns spent public funds earmarked for road repair and bridge construction to build outsized gyms instead. Soon nearly all the big gyms in the United States were in Indiana. New Castle, Elkhart, Michigan City, Lafayette—these were just some of the Indiana communities that built high school gyms that would hold seven thousand fans or more. These weren't multipurpose community centers; they were basketball palaces. During one 1929 meeting, the Muncie, Indiana, city council allocated $100,000 to build a basketball fieldhouse that would seat 7,400 fans—and then refused to put up $300 to hire a librarian.

Gym Crazy

The gymnasium construction craze continued throughout the twentieth century. By 1993, all but one of the fifteen largest high school gyms in the United States (by seating capacity) were located in Indiana:

1. New Castle, Indiana: 9,314
2. Anderson, Indiana: 8,996
3. Seymour, Indiana: 8,110
4. Richmond, Indiana: 8,100
5. East Chicago, Indiana: 8,050
6. Marion, Indiana: 7,560
7. Dallas, Texas: 7,500
8. Elkhart, Indiana: 7,373
9. Michigan City, Indiana: 7,304
10. Gary West, Indiana: 7,217
11. Lafayette, Indiana: 7,200

Winning tournament games became everything to Hoosiers. It was the way to put your school on the map, the way to gain respect. Town merchants rewarded winning high school coaches with bonuses—in one case a Pontiac sedan. Winning players got gold watches. Coaches combed the hills and flatlands for any tall boy who could shoot, offering his parents well-paying jobs if they would just uproot the family and move to their town. Many players were in their

Each year during the Indiana state basketball tournament, *Indianapolis News* reporter William Fox (left) and Butler University basketball coach Paul D. "Tony" Hinkle toured the sixteen final schools in a Stutz Bearcat sports car. In some years, they raced an airplane around the state to promote the tourney. (Indiana Basketball Hall of Fame)

early twenties. Some were married. Some hadn't passed a subject in school.

The Indiana High School Athletic Association, established in 1903 to regulate high school sports in the state, stood powerless to police the monster it had created. In 1916, the IHSAA executives threw up their hands and hired a lawman to clean up the mess. Arthur L. Trester, then thirty-eight, was an obvious choice. An ex–high school principal and school superintendent, Trester was a man to whom the mechanics of power came naturally. His first move was to appoint his most trusted friends to "the Board of Control." Soon after, critics were calling them "the Board of Controlled."

By 1927, the year he met with the three black supplicants representing the new all-black Crispus Attucks High School, Arthur Trester wielded absolute power over high school sports in Indiana. Anyone accused of breaking an IHSAA rule was summoned to Trester's office for a hearing. There King Arthur sat unblinking as the accused stammered their excuses and denials through dry, trembling lips. He usually heard them out and then banned them from competition, sending them out the door with his pet slogan: "The rules are clear, and the penalties severe."

No written record of his meeting with the Big Three about Crispus Attucks High survives, but it's not hard to imagine how it went. Presumably DeFranz, Herod, and Ransom were escorted into Trester's office, shown seats, maybe offered coffee, and asked what was on their minds. Surely the Big Three made their case that success in the basketball tourney was a path to respect, which is what the Attucks student body needed. It was, they likely pointed out, only fair and democratic and American to give Attucks a chance.

But Trester had little to gain by admitting Attucks High to the state basketball tourney in the Indianapolis of 1927. Opposition would

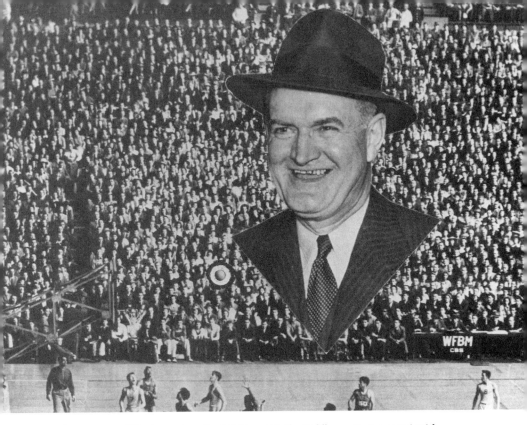

Arthur Trester and his show palace, the 15,000-seat Butler Fieldhouse. Dr. James Naismith, the inventor of basketball, watched the 1925 tourney at Butler and wrote, "The possibilities of basketball there were a revelation to me." (Courtesy Dale Glenn)

have flared from all corners of the state. It would cost him support throughout Indiana. Besides that, Gary and Evansville, Indiana's second- and third-largest cities, were also building schools for black students only. By slamming the door loudly in Indianapolis, Trester could make his message heard by black community leaders throughout Indiana: Don't even try to get in.

Straight-faced, Trester explained to the Big Three that his hands were tied. Since Indianapolis's Crispus Attucks was not a public school—it was for black students only, and white students could not attend—there was nothing he could do to help them. The IHSAA governed public schools only. Catholic schools had the same problem. It's easy to imagine the three black leaders fuming—maybe yelling at Trester as the commissioner glanced at his pocket watch and stood.

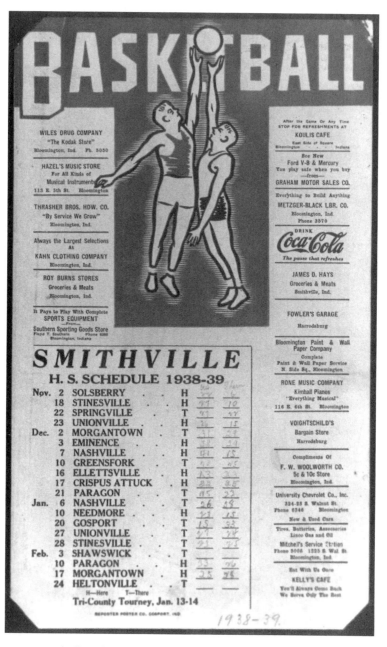

The 1938–39 Smithville High basketball schedule. Note the December 17 game against "Crispus Attuck." For fifteen years, Attucks could find games only against tiny rural schools like Smithville and against racially segregated schools throughout the Midwest. (Indiana Basketball Hall of Fame)

The rules were clear, and the penalty—for the crime of having dark skin—achingly severe.

At first, Attucks could find games only against other outcasts—all-black schools throughout the Midwest and Indiana's nine Catholic schools, also banned by Trester from the Indiana tournament. In basketball and in other sports, too, Attucks teams became nomadic, traveling amazing distances to compete, once chartering a bus from Indiana to Nebraska for a football game.

The first breakthrough came in 1933, when Attucks's principal, Dr. Russell Lane, convinced the athletic director of Ellettsville High, a small-town school north of Bloomington, to take a chance on a game with Attucks. As a precaution, Elletsville's athletic director wrote to Trester seeking permission.

Dr. Russell Lane

Short, bespectacled, and always tastefully dressed, Dr. Russell Lane refused to accept any notion that Crispus Attucks High, its students, or its faculty were inferior. Lane's parents were distinguished scholars who had brought their children up to believe that education was the pathway to progress. Lane took over as Attucks's principal in 1930, determined to make the school a center of excellence.

He recruited an all-star faculty, including several PhD scholars who were available only because Indiana's white schools would not hire black teachers. Many came from southern historically black colleges. One, John Morton-Finney, spoke seven languages. Dr. Lane snapped them up and developed at Attucks a rich and enormous curriculum that included subjects from college algebra to tailoring. From the very beginning, Attucks produced leaders, students who went on to become jazz pioneers, military officers, authors, historians, and teachers.

Dr. Lane, quickly realizing the overwhelming importance of basketball in Indiana, struggled to give Attucks the chance to play against other Indiana public schools.

Trester replied that he would allow IHSAA member schools to play Attucks in "contests in which not more than two schools should be involved at the same time." In other words, the big prize—the tournament—was still out. Dr. Lane chose to see Trester's decision not as a rejection, but as the first break in the clouds.

The following season brought Attucks a few more games against the tiny backwoods schools. Motor caravans formed in Attucks's parking lot on West Twelfth Street and followed two-lane roads out of Frog Island, out of Naptown, and into the starlit darkness until they reached a crossroads schoolhouse whose oversized gym blazed with light.

Rural children, gawking at the first dark-skinned people many of them had ever seen, clustered around the Attucks players as they emerged from the vehicles. Some shyly asked for autographs. "It was like we were from outer space," recalled one Attucks student. "I would hear them say, 'Look at that one . . . He's *really* black.'"

According to a former cheerleader, "Everywhere we went, folks would wait for our buses to arrive and then follow us into the gym. I remember one night this little boy came down and wanted to talk to the cheerleaders. He was a friendly little lad and we had a good chat. He stayed right with us through the start of the game, and a few minutes into the contest I felt this scratching at my arm. I turned and looked, but I didn't see anything. A little later there it was again. That little boy was scratching my arm with his fingernail and then putting it into his mouth. 'It isn't chocolate,' I told him. 'It's my skin, the same as yours. I'm just darker than you are.'"

To many white fans, the Attucks players were like the Harlem Globetrotters, entertainers who had come to play an exhibition. But the games meant something quite different to Principal Lane. He viewed each backwoods gym as a showcase for progress and each Attucks player a goodwill ambassador. A game at a rural schoolhouse was a chance to demonstrate to white fans, some of whom doubtless still had robes and hoods stashed in their closets, that black and white Hoosiers could compete without violence or incident. If Hoosiers could observe racial harmony while their sons competed in a packed gym, Lane thought, they would later come to believe in its possibility in schools and neighborhoods.

The Harlem Globetrotters

The 1950–51 team, with owner and coach Abe Saperstein on the far right. (Wikimedia Commons)

The Harlem Globetrotters were—and still are—an exhibition basketball team that combines athletic prowess, theater, and comedy. Globetrotter teams have come to represent the flair of basketball as played by many African Americans. Some have accused the team of pandering to racial stereotypes by presenting black players not as competitors, but as clownish entertainers, as pranksters. However, "the Globies," as they sometimes call themselves, have rarely lost a game against their traditional foes, the Washington Generals.

At its founding in 1926, the team consisted mainly of players from Chicago's Wendell Phillips High School. Since then, the Globetrotters have played more than twenty-six thousand exhibition games in 123 countries and territories. Brother Bones's whistled version of "Sweet Georgia Brown," the team's theme song, is known throughout the world.

In the years during which Crispus Attucks High could find games only in rural Indiana communities, the Globetrotters were the only black players most white fans had ever seen or even heard of. And in the years before 1951, when the first African American players joined the rosters of National Basketball Association (NBA) teams, winning a spot on the Globetrotters was the ultimate ambition for young black men who sought to earn a living playing basketball. The first three African American NBA players—Charles "Tarzan" Cooper, Nat "Sweetwater" Clifton, and Earl Lloyd—had all played on Globetrotter squads. The Globetrotters staged giant tryouts in locations across the nation, attracting hundreds of hopefuls, only a very few of whom were offered contracts by the Globies.

Dr. Lane personally oversaw the choice of players on the Attucks basketball team. He selected polite, well-spoken boys who didn't anger quickly. Lane constantly lectured his players not to commit fouls or protest referee calls. He insisted that the players ignore taunts and do their best to avoid physical contact. They were to forget about showboat passes and behind-the-back dribbling. They were *not* the Harlem Globetrotters. As representatives of their race, they were to behave with dignity.

Once the games began, Lane worked his way through the bleachers, introducing himself to farmers and shop owners and housewives. Many found themselves warming to the short, bespectacled, genial man in a suit and tie who reached out for their hands and chatted with them until the final buzzer sounded, at which time he would shepherd his players, still glistening with sweat, out of the gymnasium.

But sometimes it was hard for even Dr. Lane to remain buoyant. They were so poor. Attucks's players dressed in hand-me-down uniforms salvaged from a throwaway pile at Butler University. Students did their best to patch them up in the high school's tailoring shop, but the patchwork showed. They sometimes practiced on the stage of the school's theater, where a scramble for a loose ball could send players tumbling over the lip and into the front row of seats. Without a gym, Attucks could not host other schools. Every game was an away game.

And at those other schools, some officials wouldn't even let Attucks players shower in their locker rooms after a game. Diners that would serve meals to black patrons had to be scouted out in advance. And because no rural motel would accept black guests, team members had to drive straight home after the games or else sleep in a local flophouse or YMCA. Sometimes they slept on gym floors.

But worst of all was not being able to play in the state tourney. March would roll around each season, and while the other Indianapolis schools were holding pep rallies, Attucks's players were cleaning out their lockers. Year after year, the Big Three, along with a growing number of black and Catholic leaders and white liberals, crusaded for the admission of Indiana's black and parochial schools to the IHSAA. And year after year, Arthur Trester and his Board of Controlled just seemed to set their stubborn jaws a little tighter.

It all came to a head at a meeting of the Indianapolis school board one evening early in 1941. F. E. DeFranz, one of the Big Three who had attended the very first meeting with Trester, rose to launch yet another passionate appeal for the board's support of the outcast schools' bid to compete in the tournament. DeWitt Morgan, the board's superintendent, cut him off sharply. "I am sorry, DeFranz," Morgan snapped. "Not in my time nor in your time will this happen."

But Morgan was mistaken. That very March, Indiana legislator Robert Brokenburr introduced Senate Bill 181, calling for state regulation of Arthur Trester's ISHAA and the admission of black and Catholic schools. In those passionate days, with America's entry into World War II just around the corner, church leaders joined the fight. They decried the hypocrisy of denying opportunities to black students who would soon be asked to risk their lives for freedom. Editorial support in the *Indianapolis Star* gave the bill momentum. It passed the Senate handily, and only a parliamentary maneuver kept it from passing in the House.

On December 20, 1941, just two weeks after the United States declared war against Japan, Arthur Trester issued a matter-of-fact order opening the ISHAA to all "public, private, parochial, colored, and institutional high schools of the state offering and maintaining three or four years of high school work."

After fifteen years of struggle, at last the outcast schools had a chance.

Bailey, Henry, and Oscar Robertson arrived in Indianapolis from Tennessee with their mother in 1942, the very year that Attucks was first allowed to play in the tournament. After a year of crowded living in the home of his sister Inez, Bailey Robertson Sr. found a four-room house at 1005 Colton Street in Frog Island.

"The place was your standard shotgun shack," Oscar Robertson later wrote. "Its rooms joined in a straight line that you could look through, and the roof was made of tar paper—just strong enough to protect us from rain, but too flimsy to shelter us from cold, windy nights or flies and mosquitoes. There was running water, but the toilet was outside. A big potbelly stove sat smack-dab in the middle of the house [but] even with the potbelly stove, there was no heat in the wintertime. You would get under all the covers you could, but the wind would come right through the windows. You would hear [neighbors] arguing and fighting all the time. And gunshots at night."

The house was situated in a notoriously tough part of Frog Island that would become known as Kinkaid's Hole. The nickname came from a western movie titled *Bandits of the Badlands*, which reached the neighborhood's Lido Theatre in the mid-1940s. In the movie, a

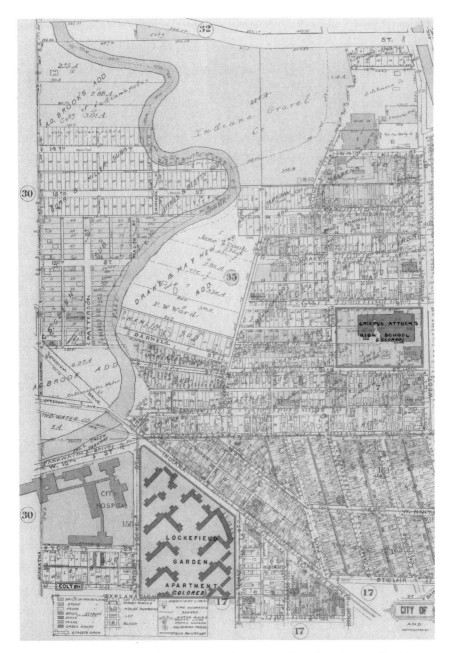

Detail from a 1941 street atlas of Indianapolis. Colton Street, where the Robertsons lived, is at the bottom left. Both Attucks High School and Lockefield Gardens were designated "Colored." (IUPUI University Library digital collections)

posse of Texas Rangers chases a gang of cattle thieves right into the gang's hideout. After a lot of tough talk, they decide to settle the matter with their fists. One outlaw dressed in black and one Ranger dressed in white jump down into a ladderless pit known as Kinkaid's Hole, where they slug out their differences. The name stuck in Frog Island. Kinkaid's Hole was the toughest spot in the neighborhood. And this was just where Bailey, Henry, and Oscar Robertson were now living.

The three Robertson boys played basketball in an alley behind their house because that's all there was to do and all that anyone did. Bailey cut the bottom from a peach basket and nailed it to a tree. They called it their "dust bowl," the common name for unpaved basketball courts in the neighborhood. Having no basketball, they made a ball of rags held together by elastic, or stuffed newspaper into a rolled-up sock tied with string, and pretended they could bounce it. They practiced day and night, playing imaginary games that Bailey, the oldest and biggest, dominated. "We taught one another," Bailey later recalled. "You just kept shooting, even in the dark. Your eyes adjusted. I played a lot in the dark."

The best basketball competition in Frog Island was found at Lockefield Gardens, just around the corner from Kinkaid's Hole. Lockefield Gardens was a 748-unit federal housing project whose twenty-four buildings were filled with modern, three-room apartments. It had everything: hot and cold running water, steam heat, indoor plumbing, electric stoves and refrigerators, hardwood floors, a central courtyard, barber and beauty shops, and even a theater. If you were black, it was the best place to live in Indianapolis.

But for Frog Island boys, Lockefield's main attraction was a rectangle of worn asphalt separating two netless basketball goals at the margin of a playground. The court was rarely empty. There, even on snow-swept winter evenings and sweltering summer days, Frog Island warriors played a bruising form of basketball that bore little resemblance to the delicately patterned game whites learned in school programs elsewhere in Indiana.

The Lockefield basketball court became an obsession for all three Robertson boys, but because he was older, Bailey got the first chance to play in the showcase weekend games. It was a great honor to be chosen for a team at Lockefield, since that meant your teammates counted you an asset. The house rules were starkly simple: *First team to 20 points wins, with each basket counting for 2 points. No overtime. Win and stay in. Lose and get lost.* If you lost, it could take all day to get back for a second chance. Arguments sometimes became loud and physical.

Proud and sensitive, Bailey was a cocky player, taunting and aggressive, who stayed in your face to let you know he was on top. But even more, he was a great shooter, one who took a hard dribble, stopped, and leaped high for his one-handed shot. His exaggerated follow-through gave him the neighborhood name "Flap." He shot all the time, which sometimes annoyed his teammates. Still, it was widely agreed that Flap Robertson was the guy you would want to take a pressure shot with the game on the line.

Oscar was too young and too small to get in the big games, but he hung out at the Lockefield court anyway, studying the older players, soaking up their moves and strategies, peppering them with questions between their games. Having no basketball of his own, he snatched up the players' ball between games to get in a few shots before the giants demanded it back.

Oscar played at Lockefield when the court was available—usually when it was too hot or too cold—and when anyone had a basketball they were willing to share. Sometimes he played with friends, sometimes by himself. When there was no ball available, he practiced his fakes and moves alone on the Lockefield court. "At least I always knew where he was," his mother later explained.

Though Oscar was slender and light, his game was advanced from the very beginning. One neighbor named Harold Andrews, who went by the name "440," remembered a game of three-against-three involving the young Oscar. "I was about seventeen," 440 recalled. "Oscar was about nine . . . They all said, 'You take Palmer'—that's what they called him. Palmer—it was his middle name. The kid just wore me out. I said, 'I ain't takin' Palmer no more.'"

Oscar Robertson heard it again and again: He was too small, too young, too light. His time was still years away.

At least that's how he was thinking when a miracle swept him up like a tornado and dropped him into a faster lane. Bailey and Henry were stunned when, one Christmas morning, Oscar opened a gift-wrapped box and lifted out a basketball. All three boys stared at it in disbelief. Oscar had begged his mother for a ball, but Bailey and Henry hadn't taken the begging seriously or bothered to ask for a ball of their own, because a basketball was clearly beyond the family's budget. Where had their mother come up with that kind of money?

Beaming, Mazell explained that the lady she cleaned for had asked her what each of her sons wanted for Christmas. She had dutifully reported that Oscar wanted a ball and was amazed when the lady handed over her son's old ball. The lady said she had been meaning to get her son a new one anyway.

To Bailey and Henry, *how* it had gotten there didn't matter. What mattered was that it was *Oscar's* ball. Oscar was now not only the sole basketball owner in the family, but the sole private ball owner in the entire *neighborhood*.

Oscar made it clear to Bailey and Henry that it was not the Robertson family ball, just his. He took it out the door with him in the morning and carried it wherever he went. At night, sometimes with Bailey looking on hungrily, Oscar soaped down the ball and placed it carefully beside their bunk bed before closing his eyes. Many years later, after he had made his name as one of basketball's all-time greats, Oscar Robertson could still remember the ball in detail. "It was sort of scarred up," he said. "Old. Didn't have the greatest trim on it. But then again, the tread wasn't lopsided, and the ball was regulation size."

Bottom line?

"It was my ball."

Ray Crowe, eldest of eight boys in a family of eleven children, was one of Indiana's outstanding young athletes in his day. He was mild-mannered by nature, but he played a bruising style of basketball. (University of Indianapolis Archives and Special Collections)

Ray Crowe: "I Would Love to Meet Your Family"

This is what made coaching so wonderful. So awful, too. It was giving to kids, giving everything you had, your experience, your knowledge, your life, yourself. Then sending them out into the world while you sat and looked on and suffered with them and for them.

—John R. Tunis, *Yea! Wildcats!*

In 1931, **Whiteland High School's** fifteen-year-old freshman guard, Ray Crowe, was usually the youngest player and the only player of color on the court. Opponents pushed him around and taunted him with racial slurs, testing his self-confidence and challenging his toughness. Crowe backed away and held his tongue only because that's what he thought his coach, Glen Ray, expected of him. Still, foes found it unsettling to confront this powerfully built young man who yielded ground, but only as he was looking at you without blinking and as the muscles in his jaws popped in and out around his clenched teeth.

One Friday night, at the halftime of a game against Whiteland's archrival, Franklin High, Coach Ray took his young guard aside for a private talk. Franklin's star guard, Zion McGlocklin, had been shoving Crowe all over the court in the first half, and Whiteland had fallen steadily behind. "Listen to me," the coach said. "I don't care what color you are, but if you let yourself get pushed around any more, you're going to be watching this game from the bench. Understand?"

Big Dave DeJernett

Unlike Indianapolis, most Indiana communities allowed blacks and whites to study together in the same school building. As years passed, more and more blacks played on their high school teams with whites. The first black star was Robert David "Big Dave" DeJernett, a powerfully built center who in 1930 became the first black player to play on an Indiana state championship team. He was Ray Crowe's hero.

Dave grew up in Washington, a railroad town in southeastern Indiana. In 1930, Dave's Washington Hatchets drew Vincennes High School as their opponent in the opening game of the state tourney's sectional round. A few days before the game, the school office received a letter addressed to Dave. The writer threatened to kill Dave if he "so much as touched" a certain white Vincennes player during the upcoming game. It was signed "Committee of fourteen, KKK."

Dave was permitted to play, but on game day his dad packed a loaded

Robert David "Big Dave" DeJernett, Indiana's first prominent black high school player, soars to collect a rebound.
(Indiana Basketball Hall of Fame)

pistol up to the top row of the Vincennes gym and kept his hand on it as he scanned the crowd throughout the game. There was no attempt on Dave's life, and Washington won easily. The Hatchets kept rolling through the tournament, routing Muncie Central 32–21 in the final game. Big Dave DeJernett became the first African American in U.S. history to lead a racially integrated team to a major tournament championship. His achievement was reported in news media as far away as China.

The words from his coach were music to Ray Crowe's ears. He had had enough. When play resumed, Zion McGlocklin started right in with a hearty push. Ray took a step forward, put two hands on the boy's chest to drive him backward, advanced a step and shoved him harder, and then, before an astonished crowd and a delighted coach, chased Franklin's McGlocklin up into the bleachers. "I think he got the message," Ray Crowe later recalled, "because he played me fair after that."

Respect all, but back down from no one—here was a life lesson Ray could live by. He would later pass it on to the players he would coach at Crispus Attucks High. Ray's showdown with McGlocklin would be reflected in the tough, aggressive, but fair-minded style for which his Attucks players were known and praised.

Eldest son in a family of eleven children—eight boys—Ray Crowe grew up on a farm in Whiteland, Indiana, about twenty miles south of Indianapolis. The Crowes were one of only two black families in all of Johnson County. Thoughtful and soft-spoken, young Ray made friends easily but sometimes found it hard to sort through the conflicting signals that governed just how assertive a black boy could be in the county. While Ray enjoyed laughing and joking and playing ball with his white pals, the group knew there were certain things they couldn't do together. Ray couldn't sit with them in the main section at the movie theater in Franklin—he had to climb the stairs to the balcony and watch by himself. He couldn't swim with his friends in the town pool, and the Crowe family couldn't dine in Franklin's restaurants, where it was clear they were unwelcome. Ray and his friends never spoke about these differences, but they were in the air.

On Saturday nights when the Crowe family went into Franklin to shop, there were always men in white robes and cone-shaped hats clustered around the town square. Some waved traffic around as if they were cops. Others loitered on the courthouse steps, laughing and smoking and trying to look necessary. Ray's parents struggled to explain the Ku Klux Klan to their children. "You don't have to be afraid," they said. Ray wasn't. Inside the flimsy hoods were men Ray worked with side by side each year in the fields at harvesttime. Every autumn his family shared harvest dinners with these same guys. What was there to be afraid of?

When he was little, Ray worked long hours with his dad in the fields as winter gave way to spring, rising at dawn to plow soil into straight, dark rows, plant seeds, and then tend the crops they would harvest in the autumn. He listened obediently to his father's sermons about what he was doing wrong, and he tried not to make the same mistakes twice. Along the way, he developed a deep dislike for farm work. When he was old enough to start school, he quit farming and never looked back.

By then, like so many other Hoosier boys, Ray Crowe had fallen in love with basketball. He started out shooting baskets at a goal in a neighbor's hayloft. Dissatisfied with this setup, he built his own goal in the Crowe barnyard, next to the chicken coop. He attached wheels to the frame so he could push it away from a spot too puddled with rainwater or carpeted with soggy feathers. The Crowe family's portable goal became the place to play around Whiteland.

Athletic, intensely competitive, and lightning fast, Ray Crowe starred on Whiteland's grade school and junior high teams, then became a starting guard on the varsity basketball team as soon as he reached high school age. His coach, Glen Ray, admired Ray's leadership ability and encouraged him to ask strategic questions about how the game of basketball was played.

In March 1931, the coach took Ray and several Whiteland teammates to the state high school tournament at Butler Fieldhouse in Indianapolis. It was the semi-final round, the Sweet Sixteen, in which games would be played consecutively—morning till night—to determine which team would represent central Indiana in the final four. The Whitelanders packed food for the whole day and set off in the early morning for Indianapolis.

Barn-shaped, redbrick Butler Fieldhouse rose before them like a palace as the group hiked through long rows of Model-T Fords in the parking lot. Outside the building were dozens of radio trucks bearing call letters of stations from all over central Indiana. Back home, their Whiteland classmates would be begging teachers to please let them listen to the broadcasts during lunch hour and study halls. The

Butler Fieldhouse in the 1930s. (University Archives, Butler University Libraries)

teachers would likely give in, reasoning that the games were all the students would be thinking about anyway.

Scalpers clustered outside the gates, asking high prices for tickets. Ignoring them, the boys and their coach joined the herd and pushed their way into the giant building. They jostled along a dim corridor filled with fans, many carrying hot coffee in one hand, until they reached their gate. Then Ray Crowe, who would someday be regarded by many as the greatest high school coach in Indiana history, stepped into Butler Fieldhouse for the first time.

It was a single enormous room filled with light and sound and motion. Long shafts of sunlight poured down through mammoth windows at the top, striking the basketball court and flooding it with light. Steeply rising rows of silver bleacher seats tapered into a faraway dimness. At courtside, long tables supported dozens of typewriters, over which fedora-wearing newspaper reporters bent themselves and clattered out their first stories of the day. Cheerleaders pranced around the floor. School bands played fight songs. Students in letter sweaters waved penants. The colossal building buzzed with anticipation. The Whitelanders tromped up to their row and scooted to their seats. By the tip-off of the first morning game, every one of the great room's fifteen thousand seats was occupied. With all the pools of light and no columns to obstruct sight lines, there was not a bad seat in the fieldhouse.

They didn't get home until late that night. The impression of his first visit to Butler never left Ray Crowe. From then on, he wanted to coach high school basketball. He understood the game strategically and even as a young player had a gift for motivating his teammates. He loved to be around them. After graduating from Whiteland High, Ray was offered an athletic scholarship to Indiana Central College (ICC), a small college in Indianapolis.

Ray was again one of a very few black students at the school and, after his freshman year, the only black player on the basketball team. There were the usual problems. An opponent from Hanover College cocked a fist in Ray's face and addressed him with a racial slur; his teammates rushed to the floor to stand as one for Ray. A restaurant in southern Indiana refused to serve the ICC team because of Ray's presence; Coach Harry Good ordered his players back into their cars and led them to a restaurant in central Indiana he knew would welcome them. Loyalty was everything.

Ray flourished at ICC. He was a fine student—especially in math—and the college's star athlete. During one track meet in his sophomore year, he finished first in the 100-yard dash, the 220-yard dash, the broad jump, the low hurdles, and the shot put. He came within two points of outscoring the entire opposing team by himself.

In 1938, Ray graduated with honors but could not find a teaching job. The problem was that no white principal in Indiana would hire a black teacher, leaving hundreds of well-qualified black teachers to compete for the few jobs available at Indiana's segregated schools. Crispus Attucks High, where Ray had done his student teaching, was overcrowded and had substandard facilities, but its faculty was filled with distinguished scholars who had earned advanced degrees at fine colleges—basically, they were professors who couldn't get jobs at colleges or universities. Ray swept floors at a trucking company as he applied for teaching positions, though with increasing pessimism. He told himself that there was no point in becoming bitter and that he was lucky just to have any job at all.

In 1945, he was offered a position as a seventh- and eighth-grade math instructor at Booker T. Washington Public School 17, the junior high school next door to Attucks High. On the first day of school, Ray arrived early and stood by himself across the street from P.S. 17, watching the students laughing and chasing each other across the lawn before the bell rang. He felt deeply uncomfortable, and he knew why. "I had never seen so many black kids in all my life," he recalled. "It was sort of a shock. Being with so many blacks, and living with blacks and understanding blacks. It was different. I had grown up like a white kid."

When the bell rang, he went inside the school and wrote his name on the board for his math students. He was dressed in a neatly pressed suit with a wide, double-breasted coat and pleated trousers. His mustache was freshly trimmed. Girls found his quiet manner and soulful brown eyes attractive. Boys sized him up as a pushover. He opened his lesson plan for the day and began.

Some of the eighth-grade boys were already in their late teens, streetwise, and a head taller than their new teacher, Mr. Crowe. When Crowe turned his back to them to write on the blackboard, they snickered out loud, passed notes, and zipped paper airplanes around the classroom. A few openly mocked him, becoming ever bolder when he didn't respond. Day by day it got worse. Crowe thought about quitting. He sought advice from other teachers. The shop teacher carved him a paddle and told him to use it. But Crowe didn't want to beat his students—why should a student have to be smacked into an education? As the first weeks wore on and students became bolder, he wrote out a letter of resignation but could not quite bring himself to hand it to the principal. He was in anguish.

Hallie Bryant, who later became one of Ray Crowe's star basketball players at Attucks, remembers a showdown: "One math class, Ray left the room and then came back. This guy was showin' off for the girls. He had a navy cap on. Hats were against the rules, but he kept it on when Ray came back in. Ray didn't say anything, but he sat up very straight at his desk and you could see the muscles in his jaws poppin' out.

"This guy kept at it. After a while Ray rose and very calmly walked to him, took the cap off his head, stood him up by the collar, and whapped him horizontally across the face, vertically across the face, and then whapped a little circle around his head. Then he stuffed the guy in his seat. No one made a sound. The kid sniffled, 'I'm gonna bring my daddy, I'm gonna bring my uncle.' Ray said, 'Please bring them *all*. I would love to meet your family.'"

With no junior high basketball program in Indianapolis, Ray Crowe organized an after-school intramural basketball program for his students. He saw at once that they knew nothing about how to play the game. Ray had started playing on organized school teams in Whiteland in sixth grade, but none of these boys had worn a uniform or even heard a referee's whistle. That partially explained why, after thirty-six years of tournament play, no team from Indianapolis, by far the state's largest city, had ever won the state tournament. Indianapolis players started playing too late, played against weaker competition, and were coached by men who had too little knowledge of the game. And the boys had no basketball heroes. Who was there to look up to? Crispus Attucks High usually lost in its first-round tournament games. The Indianapolis Olympians, a pro team, had no black players. The Harlem Globetrotters were highly entertaining, but they were true globetrotters—they traveled around the world and only made it to Indiana perhaps twice a year.

Crowe's P.S. 17 students swarmed to his intramural program after school. He began each session with calisthenics and then divided the boys into basketball teams. At first they just banged each other around and complained that they'd been fouled. But day by day, Crowe taught them the fundamentals of team basketball, and they began to respond. During breaks from basketball, he dazzled them with handsprings, backflips, and other gymnastic moves. Mr. Crowe's signature trick was the talk of the school. "He used to run up the wall, spring off it, and slam dunk a basketball," remembers Hallie Bryant. "That really used to impress us little kids."

Crowe visited the homes of his students and was shocked by the living conditions in Frog Island. Many of the houses provided only crude shelter. "[Some houses were] shacks sitting along the edge of the canal," Crowe later wrote. "Many had cinders for floors, no heat and no electricity. Some housing was nothing more than a few sheets of corrugated metal nailed to two-by-fours . . . It was disappointing to see people living in such squalid conditions, but they still had a dignity about themselves . . . they didn't want pity."

Crowe recognized that there was great athletic talent in his after-school group; the boys had just never had a chance to express it. Three students stood out in particular. Willie Gardner, an introverted boy with the strange nickname "Dill," stood nearly a head taller than anyone else in his class. But there was nothing awkward about him; in fact, he had the coordination of a gymnast. Fooling around one day, Mr. Crowe demonstrated a standing back handspring and challenged the boys to try. Willie was the only one who could do it. And he did it again and again.

Another great talent was Hallie Bryant, who took to basketball immediately. An amazing one-handed shooter, Hallie was slashing and fearless with the ball. He seemed to be able to leap into the air, fold his legs beneath him, and hang there forever, tucking the ball out of reach and delaying his shot until his defenders returned to earth. Yet he was a sensitive boy whose self-confidence could deflate suddenly. One teacher's casual remark that he shot too much sent Hallie to Coach Crowe in tears. "Mr. Crowe sat me down and said, 'I'm your coach, and I want you to shoot.' He visited my home and got to know my parents," Hallie recalled. "He became like one of our family."

Then there was Bailey "Flap" Robertson. A brash, fiery competitor, Flap was a player whom Crowe found hard to reach. Bailey and his brothers had moved with their parents into the house on Colter Street, but their true address was still the neighboring dust-bowl court at Lockefield Gardens. They were there all the time. Through countless outdoor games, Bailey had developed into a brilliant shooter. Other parts of his game were unpolished, but no one in Frog Island could outshoot Flap Robertson.

Willie Gardner, Hallie Bryant, and Flap Robertson: three boys at the apex of young African American talent in Indianapolis, talent that had been suppressed too long. Now it was about to explode. Ray Crowe, at last comfortable in the classroom and admired throughout the Frog Island community, was glad he had not quit teaching during those tough early days. There was a sense that someday he would coach these young boys, and they wanted with all their hearts to impress him. "He'd come into the neighborhood dressed sharp, had a tie on," Hallie Bryant recalls. "He'd say, 'I was wondering who's gonna play for me next year? Am I gonna have a corner shooter?' Man, after he left we *lived* in that corner."

The harvest of talent was almost ready, and Crowe found it exciting. "I'd been around sports all my life and I could tell a good athlete when I saw one," he later recalled. "And now I was seeing great athletes every day."

Coach Ray Crowe chalking a play on the Attucks gym floor during practice. The players, from left to right, are Willie Posely, Harold Crenshaw, Hallie Bryant, Cleveland Harp, and Bailey Robertson. (*Indianapolis Recorder* Collection, Indiana Historical Society)

Gentlemen or Warriors?

The first mighty surge of Ray Crowe's Tigers, in 1951, aroused probably the greatest demonstration of genuine good-feeling between whites and Negroes since the Civil War. Many white people, who had been going along in the ancient ruts of prejudice, for the first time in their lives expressed a feeling of enthusiasm for these Negro youths. And many Negroes discovered for the first time that white people have hearts.

—*Indianapolis Recorder*

I n 1948, **Crispus Attucks High** School's principal, Russell Lane, offered Ray Crowe a teaching position. He was to teach math and physical education, and also to be the assistant coach for the Tigers, the varsity basketball team.

Attucks had been playing in the state tourney for five years by then, but the team had never gotten past the second game of the sectional round. Many blamed the team's head coach, Fitzhugh Lyons, who had been handpicked by Principal Lane to model good sportsmanship above all else.

Under Lane's watchful eye, Lyons taught his Attucks players a polite competitive style that some likened to ballroom dancing. They were never to leave their feet when shooting, and they were to shoot with two hands, not one. They walked the ball down the court and passed it around deliberately, probing for a clear shot. They practiced a genteel style of defense in which players guarded zones rather than individuals. They never complained, even when referees—all of whom were white—were unjust. They quickly raised their hands when fouls were called to politely indicate they were the guilty party. *Indianapolis Star* reporter Bob Collins remembers, "One time there was a collision under the basket and all five Attucks players raised their hands. They were conditioned to the fact that they were going to get cheated. Turned out [the refs] called the foul on the other team."

All the decorum got them nowhere. The Tigers were not ready to succeed in tournament play. During the pre-tournament season, most Indianapolis schools still refused to compete against Attucks. Instead of developing crosstown rivalries, Attucks continued to compete only against other black and Catholic schools, sometimes traveling hundreds of miles away. They felt like outcasts.

"I remember one little school we beat so bad even I felt sorry for them," recalled Bailey Robertson. "It was Pine Village. We beat 'em 99 to 9. They scheduled us as a sideshow. It was the first time they'd ever seen that many blacks in their lives. When the game was over we were still sweating, but they wouldn't allow us to shower. We walked across this little bridge, got back on the bus, and ate sandwiches to school, changed, and went home. Being treated that way, the names we were called, we just punished those teams."

Shooting with One Hand

During the 1940s, the technique of shooting underwent a revolutionary change. During basketball's first decades, players heaved up "set shots," stopping to get into shooting position before launching the ball. Shooters placed two hands on the ball, steadied their feet, and pushed the ball chest-out toward the hoop. But by the 1940s, a few pioneers, such as high-scoring Stanford University star Hank Luisetti, began to shoot on the run, leaping into the air and using only one hand for shooting.

When Hallie Bryant first saw a high school player leap in the air and fire off a shot with one hand, he was instantly hooked. While Fitzhugh Lyons forbade Attucks varsity players from shooting one-handed, Ray Crowe encouraged Hallie to practice it in junior high and as a freshman. To Crowe, the running one-hander took full advantage of Hallie's speed, daring, and coordination. When Crowe took over the Attucks Tigers, Hallie's one-hander was unleashed. Soon players throughout the city were trying to shoot like Hallie Bryant.

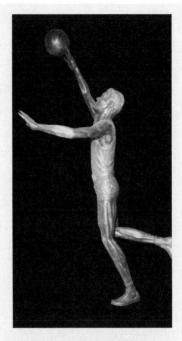

A statue on display at Stanford memorializes Hank Luisetti's revolutionary one-handed shot.
(Chuck Painter/Stanford News Service)

Late in the 1950 season, Fitzhugh Lyons resigned abruptly. He cited health issues, but it was widely believed he had been hounded out of the job by intense community pressure to make a winner of Attucks in the state tournament. "What good is all the trouble we went to, to play in the tourney," fans grumbled, "when you get beat right away year after year?"

Ray Crowe agreed. He was especially disgusted by one comment he'd overheard Lyons make after Ben Davis High easily eliminated

Attucks in the first round of the 1950 Indianapolis sectional tourney. "Oh, well," Lyons had muttered, "we might as well lose now as later."

Following Lyons's resignation, Dr. Lane appointed Ray Crowe head coach of the Attucks varsity. If Crowe had a philosophy about achieving racial progress through basketball, it was that everyone would gain from winning. Winning players would gain self-respect. The black community would draw strength from a proud winning team. And whites would respect warriors who carried themselves with pride. *Respect all, but back down from no one.* It was the lesson he had learned in Whiteland when he chased Zion McGlocklin into the bleachers.

The team he fielded in 1950 was a hybrid of his intramural players—tough, poor, southern-born kids from Frog Island like Hallie Bryant, Willie Gardner, and Flap Robertson—mixed with a group of holdovers from Fitzhugh Lyons's team. The two groups represented conflicting philosophies within the faculty at Crispus Attucks High School, within the black community of Indianapolis, and in black America in general. In many ways, the 1950—51 Crispus Attucks High basketball season was about whether to make progress by behaving as gentlemen or as warriors.

Fitzhugh Lyons and Russell Lane had stocked the Attucks teams with the well-behaved sons of the small black middle class in Indianapolis, young men who could be counted on to control their tempers in competition. The Frog Island boys scornfully called them "Northsiders."

These contrasting philosophies were embodied in the two tallest players on the Attucks varsity. Bob Jewell, the starting center, had been Russell Lane and Fitzhugh Lyons's pet project.

A six-five senior, Jewell was a fine shooter and rebounder, scholarly and reflective by nature. The student council president, Jewell was probably the most respected student at the school. His parents were together, and both worked and had scraped up enough money to pay for a home in a white North Side neighborhood. Jewell's older sister had been a top scholar at Attucks. The model of a scholar-athlete, Bob Jewell was Dr. Lane's Exhibit A. Ray Crowe thought he was soft.

By contrast, Willie Gardner, a forward at six-eight, often came to school hungry. From time to time he dropped out of school to find work to help his mother, whose suffering often troubled his dreams at night. He was reed thin, loose limbed, and seemingly carefree. Sometimes in the heat of a game he would burst out laughing. Fitzhugh Lyons, who viewed Willie Gardner as an embarrassment, had taunted and mocked Gardner repeatedly during practice, making him run laps around the gym alone while the others sat and watched. "I don't know how many times he told me I'd never be a basketball player," Gardner later recalled.

But Ray Crowe knew Willie Gardner as a deeply proud and private individual, and an amazing talent.

Willie didn't join the team until Attucks's thirteenth game of the 1950—51 season. Crowe instantly inserted Willie in the starting lineup and gave him free rein to run and handle the ball. After Willie joined, the Tigers won the final eight games of the regular season by an average of 28 points.

Midway through one early game, Hallie Bryant's long jump shot bounded off the rim and went straight up. Willie Gardner, crouched beneath the basket, leaped up, cupped the ball in one hand high above the basket, and jammed it straight down through the hoop. The crowd, at first stunned, whooped with joyous appreciation. In the Indiana of 1951, that dunk was a revolutionary move, a stylistic breakthrough something like the swooping, high-flying, thunderous dunks that Julius Erving and Michael Jordan would bring years later.

Crowe let Willie work out a pregame dunking routine. First he did a left-handed dunk, then a right-handed dunk, and then a two-handed over-the-head dunk. Opposing players, especially those from the farm towns that still made up much of the Attucks schedule, would sometimes stop their own warm-up drills to gawk as Willie Gardner dunked. Smart coaches kept their players in the locker room until Attucks was finished warming up.

Attucks entered the 1951 Indianapolis sectional as slight favorites. No one could ignore their dominance or their glossy 18—1 record, but some sportswriters believed the Attucks schedule was still too weak to produce a champion. Attucks quickly showed how mistaken the pundits were: the Tigers raised all eyebrows by winning their four sectional contests against city foes by an average of 25 points.

Indiana Avenue

Indiana Avenue, 1956. The avenue was the heartbeat of cultural life for African Americans in Indianapolis. (O. James Fox Collection, Indiana Historical Society)

Indiana Avenue, an eight-block-long boulevard that sliced diagonally through Frog Island, was the center of African American work and play in Indianapolis. At one end stood the Walker Theatre, built by Madam C. J. Walker, who had become a millionaire by selling hair-care products to blacks. The four-story redbrick building held a casino, a drugstore, a beauty shop, a coffee shop, a theater, and business offices. The avenue was lined with nightclubs, grocers, tailors, pawnshops, and finance companies. Jazz artists—including Attucks graduates Wes Montgomery and Freddy Hubbard, who became jazz pioneers—developed the "Indy Sound" in the clubs along the avenue. Nearly all the jazz greats of the era played on Indiana Avenue. A black-run fire station and police post maintained order. Indiana Avenue was a place where blacks, unwelcome elsewhere in Indianapolis, created and celebrated their own rich culture.

Now Frog Island throbbed with excitement. Store windows along Indiana Avenue from City Hospital to Walker Theatre blossomed with good-luck signs for the second, or regional, round, to be played the following Saturday at Butler Fieldhouse. The tourney was televised for the first time, and during the sectional games, neighbors had clustered around TV consoles in bars and hotels, squinting to make sense of the blurry black-and-white images on tiny oval screens. In a special advertising feature, over seventy merchants placed ads in the *Indianapolis Recorder*, urging their Tigers on.

Attucks breezed through the Indianapolis sectional, winning each of four games in blowouts, and kept right on rolling the following Saturday, easily winning the opening game of the tournament's regional round.

The 1951 Indianapolis regional final on March 3, 1951, was by far the biggest game in which Crispus Attucks High School had ever played. Their opponent was the Anderson High School Indians, one of Indiana's traditional powerhouse teams. The Indians played their home games in an enormous gym called "the Wigwam," which seated nine thousand fans. Attucks, whose founders back in the 1920s had no intention that the school would ever field a team in the high school tournament, barely had a practice floor.

To Coach Crowe's annoyance, Principal Lane showed up at every practice the week before, interrupting play to orate on the importance of good sportsmanship. Crowe noticed that some of his players

A detail from two pages of ads wishing the Attucks Tigers good luck in the *Indianapolis Recorder* the week before the 1951 tourney's sectional round. (*Indianapolis Recorder*)

seemed to be suffering through these speeches, shifting from foot to foot, looking around. Bob Jewell was one who seemed raptly attentive.

The 1951 Anderson-versus-Attucks regional final turned out to be a game for the ages. "I saw the greatest high school basketball game

I've ever seen last night," began *Indianapolis Times* sportswriter Jimmie Angelopolous's account the morning after the game. "I saw a great Anderson team overcome odds in physical superiority. I saw Crispus Attucks demonstrate to critics that courage and the will to win will overcome tremendous odds and poor officiating."

Attucks opened an early 45—30 lead, but Anderson cut the margin to 8 at halftime. Anderson continued to dominate play in the second half, jumping to a 70—60 lead with less than four minutes remaining. But Hallie Bryant and Willie Gardner brought Attucks back with a furious charge, stealing the ball time after time and driving hard for the hoop. Anderson began to buckle. Crumbling, too, was a belief, widely held among whites, that black athletes would break under pressure.

With seven seconds remaining and Attucks behind by a single point, Ray Crowe called a time-out to set up a play. He also put in Flap Robertson, a five-nine sophomore reserve who had barely played in the game. The play was designed for Hallie Bryant, Attucks's best shooter, but when action resumed, it was clear that Anderson knew what was coming. Sensing that the strategy was collapsing, Flap broke for the right corner, turned to square himself in a shooting position, and received Bob Jewell's pass. With the season on the line, he leaped, shot, and scored.

It was hard to understand how Flap Robertson had gotten the chance to save his school from extinction: He had barely played in the tournament up to then; in fact, he had been left off the roster for the sectional round. Sophomores rarely made the Attucks varsity team under any circumstances, and Flap hadn't played all that much during the pre-tournament season. But Ray Crowe knew Bailey Robertson from the after-school intramural sessions back at P.S. 17, and he had seen Flap shoot at Lockefield games. For all his mouthiness, Flap was a great and fearless shooter, and now it was time for a shot.

And that's how Flap Robertson had the ball in his hands at the biggest moment of his school's athletic history and in the life of his community. Flap himself later remembered it by saying, "Ray said, 'Flap, you go in the game.' And Fate said, 'Do it, Flap' . . . And I hit a shot that put us into national acclaim."

After the Anderson game, Jimmie Angelopolous typed out a long report for the *Indianapolis Times* about the Attucks team, portraying the players as ordinary young people with typical hopes and dreams. "This might as well be the story of any basketball team—in

A newspaper cartoon captures the annual burst of hysteria among Hoosiers over the state tourney. (Indiana Basketball Hall of Fame)

Podunkville, in Quail Creek, in Twin Forks—somewhere in Indiana," he began. "The story of Crispus Attucks is simple. It is one of individual enterprise and desire to excel. It is one of hard work, perseverance, and tenacity. It is the story of boys who learned to sacrifice, to respect others and to respect themselves."

That story was revolutionary in the Indianapolis of 1951. The *Indianapolis Recorder*, the weekly newspaper aimed at black Indianapolis, wrote constantly about race relations, with the Attucks basketball team in the spotlight in sports pages, in front-page stories, and in editorials.

But the city's three general-circulation papers—the *Star*, the *Times*, and the *News*—carefully avoided mentioning race in their coverage of Attucks. Attucks was not referred to as an all-black school. Angelopolous's article had come closer to breaking the unwritten agreement than any ever had. His telephone was quickly flooded with anonymous callers delivering hateful and threatening messages. After writing a similar piece for the *Indianapolis Star*, a young reporter named Bob Collins was repeatedly branded a "Communist." But in an editorial titled "Attucks Tigers and Hoosier Democracy," the *Recorder* pointed to a "tidal wave of interracial democracy" that the Attucks wins were causing. Russell Lane, the Attucks principal, thinking of the twenty-five years it had taken Attucks to build a team that could beat a state power like Anderson, simply said, "The hand of God was on that game."

The following Saturday, the Attucks Tigers cruised through the tourney's third, or semi-final, round, routing Covington by 40 points and Batesville by 20. Headlines in the *Indianapolis Recorder* about the Tigers' two semi-final matchups on March 10, 1951, were dismissive of their opponents: ATTUCKS TIGERS GET FINALS TICKETS THE "EASY" WAY . . . TIGER SQUAD TROUNCES TROJAN QUINTET 71–31 . . . SWEEP BY BATESVILLE FOR SEMIFINAL CROWN.

Late in March, the players began to prepare for the state finals. Now they were one of only 4 teams remaining from a field that had begun a month before with 759 entrants. The Tigers carried on their shoulders the hopes and dreams not only of black Hoosiers but also of many whites in their city and beyond. One group of fans from Atlanta chartered a plane to see Crispus Attucks play in the final four. It was a burning embarrassment that no school from Indianapolis had ever won the Indiana championship. After enduring decades of ridicule, some white fans in Indianapolis jumped on the Attucks bandwagon, just to put an end to the ordeal.

Being so close to the mountaintop after so long a journey moved Dr. Russell Lane almost to tears. As the players were pulling on their green-and-gold jerseys at Butler Fieldhouse before taking the court against Reitz High of Evansville in the first game of the final four, Dr. Lane entered the locker room to address them. As usual, everyone fell silent. It was a familiar sermon: "You are representing much more than your school," he told them. "You *are* black Indianapolis. This time, the whole state is watching. More important than winning is that you must demonstrate good sportsmanship. Be gentlemen."

Willie Gardner remembers trying not to pay attention to Dr. Lane. He wanted to win more than anything. But for Bob Jewell, the speech was calming. It was what Fitzhugh Lyons had always told him, and it was what he believed. Bob was proud that he had never fouled out of a game in his life. The state tourney *was* about sportsmanship as well as winning.

The game was a walking nightmare. Attucks players were out of sync, playing in slow motion, moving as if they were drifting through a dream world. No one could hit shots, and Evansville's Reitz couldn't miss them. Bob Jewell was in a special hell. He found himself guarding the first really mobile center he had ever faced, a superb outside shooter named Jerry Whitsell. "I couldn't reach his shots," Jewell recalled. "He'd go out to the corner, out where I'd never guarded anyone before, and the ball would be up over my head before I could react."

Flying Tigers Show Ability to Cope with Opponents

Coach Ray Crowe and Joseph King watch with anxiety during the Attucks-Cathedral game during the Sectionals. (Top left)

Robert Parrish and Cleveland Harp surround a Cathedral player in the fast moving action of the Cathedral game as Holsey Hickman watches for a chance to grab the roundball. (Top right)

Willie Gardner shows his ability to get up and shoot down at the basket. (Bottom left)

Willie Gardner and Holsey Hickman team up to foil Meadows's of Tech as he attempts to score. (Lower middle)

Hallie Bryant shows his deadly one-handed jump shot. (Bottom right)

One of many pages in the Attucks High School yearbook celebrating the 1951 Tigers. (Crispus Attucks Museum, IUPUI University Library digital collections)

Attucks lost 66—59, and the season was over. Bob Jewell, blaming himself, went home alone, sank down on his bed, and sobbed. He was still crying a few hours later when Dr. Lane telephoned, ordering him back to Butler Fieldhouse to attend the state championship game that evening. There was a chance, Dr. Lane told him, that Jewell might win the Arthur L. Trester Award, given to the player on the four finalist teams who best exemplified the ideal of a scholar-athlete-citizen. It didn't matter to Lane that the award bore the name of the man most responsible for keeping Attucks out of the tourney for fifteen years. What mattered was that Bob could be the first black player to win it.

Bob Jewell pulled himself together, returned to the fieldhouse, and, when his name was called, walked onto the floor to accept the award, still fighting back tears. He felt that he had let everyone down. The math was cruel: He had scored but 6 points, and the man he was guarding had scored 19. His team had lost by 7. There was no one to talk to, no source of comfort in his reserved family, no friend or sweetheart or teammate with whom he could share his grief. Ray Crowe had not really had enough time to become his coach, and his relationship with Fitzhugh Lyons left little room for emotion. "If I could have given that award back and we had won the game, I would gladly have done it," he said softly, forty years later. "It was a Band-Aid on a gaping wound."

But regardless of the loss, the 1951 Attucks team jolted India-napolis. The miracle comeback against Anderson had made white fans curious about the Attucks players as individuals. Anyone watching closely could see that that victory was not simply the product of sheer natural athleticism. The Tigers had shown disci-pline and heart. To white fans, some Attucks players were emerging as distinctive personalities. Hallie Bryant looked to be exuberant, Willie Gardner laconic, Bailey Robertson fearless, and Bob Jewell poised.

Blacks had something important to be proud of. They had done better in the tourney than any other Indianapolis team ever had, better even than the schools that still refused to compete against them. One of Attucks's cheerleaders, Edwina Bell, had made up an anthem called the "Crazy Song" that rubbed the new world order into everyone's faces. Attucks fans would begin to sing Bell's song, swaying back and forth, once the game was firmly in hand, inserting the name of the rival school in the first lines:

Oh, Tech is rough
And Tech is tough
They can beat everybody
But they can't beat us

Hi-de-hi-de, hi-de-hi
Hi-de-hi-de, hi-de-ho
That's the skip, bob, beat-um
That's the crazy song.

The earlier the song began, the sharper the goad. Opponents down by wide margins late in the game dreaded hearing the first few strains of that song. It confirmed what they already knew: that the game was history.

And now younger kids in the Frog Island neighborhood had heroes at last. They imitated Flap Robertson's jump shot in the mirror, following through with the wrist bent sharply just like Flap himself did it. They practiced shooting one-handed like Hallie Bryant. The tallest of them tried to dunk like Willie Gardner, or at least to jump up and scrape the bottom of the rim at Lockefield. And now hundreds of black boys of all ages throughout Indiana dreamed that someday they might wear the green and gold of the Crispus Attucks Tigers.

Maybe the most single-minded of these young dreamers was

twelve-year-old Oscar Robertson. Oscar had seen his brother's epochal shot against Anderson at home on television. He had waited up that night to greet his brother but had fallen fast asleep by the time Flap's key turned the lock after a night of celebrating. It hardly mattered: Oscar wasn't the same anymore. For the first time in his life, something great and promising had happened in his neglected neighborhood.

His own brother had presented him a dream worth having.

Basketball became his life. On Saturday mornings, Oscar Robertson would hop out of his bunk, dress, take a couple swallows of soda, grab his ball, and head out the door, bouncing the ball as he walked—left-handed, right-handed, crossover—looking for something to do and someone to join him. A promising first stop was Bill Brown's window at Lockefield. Oscar's good friend remembers waking up to the hail of pebbles against his bedroom window at unearthly hours. Brown would pull up the shade and squint out at a figure backlit against the new day's glare. "It was Oscar," he said years later, "wanting me to come play."

They would go to Lockefield and play one-on-one until others would start to show up. Another frequent early attendee was Hallie Bryant, Attucks's star and Flap's friend. He became Oscar's mentor. "We'd get out there before everybody," Bryant later recalled. "Just the two of us. We played one-on-one a lot. Oscar was always asking, 'How'd you do that?' I'd show him and he could do it right away. I could see me in him. He could do anything I could do. I told people he was gonna be great."

Oscar stayed outside most of the day, sometimes taking breaks in scorching heat or finger-numbing cold to pitch horseshoes or play pool or Ping-Pong in the neighborhood or to duck into the Lockefield office to get out of the weather. Sometimes he'd walk over to the baseball diamond behind City Hospital to see if there was a game.

When the weather was bad, he took his ball and practiced indoors by himself. He dreamed up hypothetical game situations and broke down imaginary defenses. Often, a chair was his indoor foe. He faked and dribbled around the chair with his left hand, then his right. He worked on his crossover dribble, his change-of-pace step, his jab step, his head fakes and shoulder fakes. He squared off against stationary objects, backed them down, faked one way and went the other. These moves would become familiar to fans of the Big O throughout the 1960s and '70s, when many were calling him the best basketball player on earth.

Oscar Robertson's boyhood geometry was a rectangle: home, church with his family, school, and Lockefield. There were no summer arts programs or enrichment activities. No rented saxophones or piano lessons. The swimming pool at Douglass Park posted a sign that said WHITES ONLY; so did the Riverside Amusement Park with its two roller coasters, the Flash and the Thriller.

Oscar sized up the Indianapolis of his youth in his autobiography: "We couldn't go into the south side of town because it was all white. The east side was very, very tough, so we stayed away from there too. We weren't wanted downtown and didn't have money to spend there anyway, so that was out. And while some blacks lived on the north side of town, we didn't have either the money or the transportation to get there . . . Racism . . . was sort of like polluted air. I inhaled it and did not realize the damage it was doing."

Flap's geography was even plainer than Oscar's. "My whole life was Lockefield," Flap said. "I couldn't have told you where Riverside Amusement Park was. It could have been in a foreign country."

In August 1946, a city policeman named James "Bruiser" Gaines started an open competition at Lockefield, calling it the Dust Bowl Tournament. The tournament winner got $3 from Bruiser's

Panoramic view of Lockefield Gardens during a Dust Bowl Tournament game. Note the spectators who climbed trees and on playground equipment to view the action. (Indiana Basketball Hall of Fame)

own pocket. The runner-up got a cake baked by Bruiser's wife, Imogene.

The first tournament had only six teams, but as word spread, pickup fives drove to Lockefield from all over the state, cars filled with whites and blacks. Oscar Robertson latched on to his first Dust Bowl team when he was only nine years old. One of the team coaches, police officer Anthony Watkins, gave in to the boy's persistence by giving him a jersey, but he kept Oscar at the end of the bench. He tried not to look at the kid. "He wanted to play bad," Watkins remembered. "Bruiser Gaines said, 'Why don't you put Oscar in?' I said, 'Man, he's too *small*.' I feel bad about that to this day. I hope Oscar forgives me for that. I overlooked him."

The two netless hoops at Lockefield offered a classroom where you could learn things worth knowing. Lockefield offered lessons in

reach-arounds, jab steps, and stop-and-go dribbles; it also taught players how to call out and set picks. Oscar developed what he called a side-step fadeaway jump shot, releasing the ball above his head so it wouldn't be blocked by taller players. He practiced the shot day and night, from various positions on the court.

Most of all, Lockefield taught its players how to compete, and Oscar became a superb competitor. Bruiser Gaines has a vivid memory of Oscar's attachment to Lockefield. After Oscar received his own basketball at Christmas, he formed the habit of playing by himself, practicing his side step on the darkened court until well after midnight. Bleary-eyed Lockefield residents with early work schedules called Officer Gaines to complain that sleep was impossible against the constant echo of the ball. "I had to run him off the Lockefield court many a night at two or three in the morning," Gaines recalled. "I'd take my BB gun and shoot it up against the backboard. He'd hear the clicks and go on home."

Attucks students, ca. 1950. (Courtesy Crispus Attucks Museum)

A Form of Jazz

To be young, gifted, and black,
Oh what a lovely precious dream.

—Nina Simone and Weldon Irvine

Ray Crowe spent much of the summer of 1951 reliving the semi-final loss to Evansville's Reitz. Negative thoughts looped around and around in his head: He had let everyone down. His players weren't in top condition. They should have played a man-to-man defense rather than a zone. He had let Russell Lane weaken them with his locker-room speeches about sportsmanship. They hadn't been tough enough.

To everyone else, Crowe's first year at Attucks had been a

coaching miracle. The Tigers had made it to the final four even though every game had been played on the opponent's court in a big gym packed with hostile fans. Still, Attucks's final four appearance was only the fifth time in forty years that *any* Indianapolis school had made the state finals. Attucks no longer practiced on the school theater stage, but the "new" gym—built in the 1940s—was still much too small. It was only five feet from the baseline to a wall on either end. The team could use the entire court only with great caution, for fear that players running at full speed would smack into one of the walls. A few rows of bleachers on one side of the court held only about two hundred spectators, so there were no large, cheering home crowds at Attucks games. The Attucks players had already become the pride of black Indiana, and now they had added some white fans in Indianapolis who were sick of losing year after year.

Frog Island suddenly throbbed with basketball life. On any given weekend day, as many as a hundred African American boys lined the outdoor court at Lockefield Gardens, observing their heroes close up and hoping to get chosen for one of the games that percolated from sunup to sundown. Even a few intrepid white players traveled into the heart of the city to test themselves against Naptown's toughest competition.

Not that all of Crowe's problems had vanished. Being the coach of Crispus Attucks High still meant putting food in his players' bellies, keeping his players in school, monitoring their grades, and sometimes even finding clothes that would fit them. He controlled their daily schedules. All Attucks basketball players in grades nine through twelve were in Mr. Crowe's homeroom, gym class, math class, and study hall. He insisted that they maintain at least a C average, and posted their grades on his classroom bulletin board for all to see. He arranged with the school cafeteria staff to give his players at least one free meal a day. "He called us together and said, 'I don't want anybody to go all day at school without eating,'" remembered one Attucks player. "He said, 'If your mother doesn't have any food in the house, let me know.' I never went hungry."

For some, Crowe was as much a dad as a coach. For those of his players who had no father living in the household, he gave them the keys to his car when they got driver's licenses and let them wear his suits to the prom. (No one seems to have minded those suits being too short on them.) When they dropped out of school to take jobs to help feed their families, he tracked them down and calmly offered them reasons to return to Attucks, explaining that an education was the only real path to money. When his brother, George Crowe, became a major-league baseball player, Ray took the Attucks team to Cincinnati to see him play. "We sat with the ballplayers' wives," recalled Attucks guard Stanley Warren. "Right behind the screen, so close you could see the curveballs breaking. The wives would buy us hot dogs and make a fuss over us."

"I remember once, after I quit my job setting pins at a bowling alley and went back to school, Ray gave me his socks," Willie Gardner recalled. "He didn't make a big deal of it. They just showed up in my locker. He knew I needed them." It didn't matter that the socks were way too small for Willie, who was nearly a foot taller than his coach. Getting to wear the argyles that had once been carefully selected to match one of Mr. Crowe's fine suits was evidence that this great man loved Willie Gardner. That meant that Willie Gardner must be worth loving. Willie took special care of those socks. In the end, his decision to stay enrolled at Attucks wasn't even close: no job was worth as much as a place in Ray Crowe's heart.

In the days before the tryouts for the 1951—52 season, Ray Crowe wrote a philosophy to guide his work with his players. He wanted something he could refer to later on when the competition got hot.

"It [is] not my job to build basketball teams with boys," he began. "It [is] my job to build boys with basketball teams." He continued:

- Right will prevail.
- Be right without fear. Unfair victory is bittersweet.
- No team can beat you if you are right. (You are at your best when you are right.)
- No team can beat you if it is wrong.
- No team can beat you at your best. Right is unbeatable.

Nearly one hundred boys swarmed to the gym to try out for the 1951–52 team. The sheer volume of hopefuls left Crowe with heartbreaking decisions, especially given the level of talent he was seeing in the tryouts. "I think a lot of the kids I cut could have made the team at any of the other city schools," Crowe said. The hopeful candidates took to calling Crowe "Razor" because he had the power to cut them from their hopes and sever them from their dreams. "Those decisions kept me up all night," Crowe later said.

Butler Fieldhouse

In 1928, Butler University, a small Indianapolis college known mainly for its pharmacy program, built America's largest basketball fieldhouse, seating fifteen thousand. The barn-shaped redbrick structure was built to give Indiana High School Athletic Association secretary Arthur Trester a home for the Indiana state high school basketball finals. Trester gave Butler $100,000 for ten years' rent. "We sure never had any trouble building a great schedule," laughed Paul D. "Tony" Hinkle, Butler's coach at the time. "Everyone wanted to come out here and see this place."

Perhaps no building has meant more to Indiana, and perhaps none has provided a better place to watch a basketball game. The high school finals were held in Butler Fieldhouse, renamed in 1966 as Hinkle Fieldhouse, until 1971. Almost all the tournament tickets went to the high schools of Indiana, who

Butler Fieldhouse in 1947. (*Indianapolis Star/USA TODAY* Network)

honored their senior athletes with a trip to Indianapolis. Ordinary fans tried desperate measures to get in.

"People would hide in here the day before," Hinkle said a few years before his death, gesturing toward the upper reaches of the great room. "We'd have to have the police come in and sweep the fieldhouse. Once I caught a guy climbing up a drainpipe toward a window. I said, 'What are you doing up there?' and he said, 'Oh, just trying to see if I could make it.'"

Hinkle once offered Trester to install another five thousand seats for the high school tournament. "Trester just laughed," Hinkle recalled. "He said, 'No, Tony, five thousand would just make things worse. If you can figure out how to squeeze in another hundred thousand, let me know.'"

Crowe packed his 1951–52 team with Frog Islanders. Willie Gardner, Hallie Bryant, and Flap Robertson were back. The polite Northsiders of the Fitzhugh Lyons days either had graduated or were not chosen. The 1951–52 squad was born in Ray Crowe's intramural program and tempered at the Lockefield Dust Bowl. They were eager to work, hungry to compete, ready to take it all.

Crowe had attended coaching clinics during the summer to learn all he could about man-to-man defenses, in which players guarded specific players rather than zones. Now the Attucks practices were much more rigorous, with what seemed to the players to be almost endless running drills.

Sporting a well-conditioned, talented, and tenacious squad, the Tigers ran away with eighteen of their first nineteen games, most by margins of over 20 points. Crowds increased by the game. Early in the season, four members of an overflow crowd, unable to get into a sold-out game between Attucks and Cathedral High School, picked up rocks and hurled them through the windows of the Cathedral gym. The newspapers put a racial spin on the incident, since three vandals were white and one black, but the real problem was that no high school gym in Indianapolis could hold all the fans who wanted to see Attucks play.

Attucks athletic director Alonzo Watford searched desperately for a bigger venue in Indianapolis. As a last resort, he agreed to deposit $300 to rent the cavernous Butler Fieldhouse in the season's next-to-last game. He was shocked when on Wednesday, February 23, more than five thousand fans showed up at Butler for a meaningless game between Attucks and a team from Dunkirk, Indiana, a small farm town more than eighty miles from Indianapolis.

The thousands of Attucks fans who surged into the giant fieldhouse—a multitude announced as the biggest crowd ever to witness a non-tournament game in Indianapolis—got more than their money's worth. Willie Gardner bounce-passed the ball between his legs on fast breaks and hung on the rim after rebounds. Hallie Bryant broke Gardner's city one-game scoring record of 42 points, mainly because once Bryant got close to his record, Gardner, his best friend, simply refused to shoot. Attucks won 104—54. Dunkirk's players, totally outmatched, seemed as stunned by Attucks's style and skill as any fan in the giant fieldhouse.

The game was a study in contrasts. While the Dunkirk players moved around the court in cautious, probing patterns, as if there were square dances and ballads running through their heads, Attucks played a form of jazz. Players improvised their attack at high speed, based on Ray Crowe's fundamental knowledge of fast-break basketball. In Crowe's scheme, Attucks players didn't really play fixed positions. On a more traditional team, Willie Gardner, Attucks's tallest player, would have been a center. His job would have been to plod down the court, station himself at the free-throw line with his back to the basket, and wait for someone to throw him a bounce pass so he could hand the ball off to a teammate cutting by or, as a last resort, throw up a shot himself.

But Willie Gardner, the best passer on the team, ran like the wind. Why hobble him? Likewise, it made no sense to treat a player of Hallie Bryant's creativity as a forward. Instead, Crowe encouraged Bryant to attack the hoop without a set plan and wait until a defender reacted to a particular fake and presented a fatal opening. Then Bryant would score. To many, it looked natural, but each split-second decision was based on an extensive body of experience and knowledge Bryant had developed at Lockefield, at P.S. 17, and at Attucks.

Not everyone was entertained. Attucks's style of play was deeply resented by many whites. The Tigers' high-speed approach seemed to mock the wisdom white coaches had been passing down to Indiana players for three generations. Jep Cadou Jr., sports editor for

Crispus Attucks High teams forever changed the way basketball was played in Indiana. Their opponents seemed to have square dances running through their heads while Attucks played jazz—fast, soaring, and improvised over a sound structural knowledge of fast-break basketball. (*Indianapolis Recorder* Collection, Indiana Historical Society)

the *Indianapolis Star*, grumbled in print that basketball's inventor "[James] Naismith never intended [that] players with 'jumping jack legs' would be able to rewrite basketball's traditional patterns."

Indeed, Attucks players jumped when they shot the ball, and used only one hand to shoot. Sometimes an Attucks rebounder would leap high to snatch an opponent's missed shot out of the air one-handed, scoop it to a guard already in full stride, and attack their basket at high speed with three or four players running. Now the Attucks warm-up drill featured *six* players who could dunk—causing opponents to gawk rather than doing their own preparations.

The morning after the Dunkirk game, Alonzo Watford went to a bank and deposited a $300 check into a new account that he named the Attucks Athletic Fund. Attucks's share of the gate at Butler was the first profit Attucks had made in a quarter century of competition. "It seemed a strange thing to do," Watford later said, "but it sure felt good."

Attucks entered the 1952 state tourney having lost only once and was ranked third in the state by the Associated Press. The Tigers had overwhelmed their opponents by an average margin of nearly 25 points. Once again, black Indianapolis saw this as the breakthrough team that would at last win the state championship and deliver the respect they deserved.

There were some very tentative signs, tender buds popping from the trees, that the city's racial climate was starting to thaw, at least toward the athletes who wore green-and-gold letter jackets.

"We'd test the places downtown," remembers guard Stanley Warren. "You'd start out on Indiana Avenue because you knew you'd get some warm fuzzies when people would see that big yellow *A* on your letter jacket. They'd say, 'Hey, *Stanley* . . . c'mon in.' Farther on, there was a restaurant at the bus station on Illinois called Fendrick's. It was segregated, but they'd serve you if you were on the basketball team. Other places we wouldn't test—we didn't know if they'd serve us or not, but we didn't want to go through the embarrassment of being rejected."

The Attucks players were mobbed everywhere they went in Frog Island the week before the tourney began. Study was impossible. Ray Crowe moved the team members out of their homes and into the Senate Avenue YMCA, where he could control what they ate, when they slept, and whom they saw.

After squeaking by Cathedral High in the first game of the sectional, Attucks faced Indianapolis Tech High in the second-round game. Tech was Attucks's archrival, the last Indianapolis school that refused to schedule a regular-season game against the Tigers. Fistfights in the bleachers were common when the two schools met, and security was always beefed up. The contest was close all the way, and its outcome rested on a final play. With Tech leading 61—60 and forty seconds remaining, Hallie Bryant tipped in Flap Robertson's missed shot for what appeared to be the winning basket. Attucks fans erupted in joyful celebration. But the goal was waved off by an official who blew his whistle to report a foul against Attucks on the play. Tech hit two free throws and held on to win 63—60.

Another year down the drain.

Again in anguish, Ray Crowe took it out on himself. "I felt like I'd let my community and school down," he wrote. "Folks built their evenings around where and how they were going to watch and listen to our ball games. We were their pride and joy and we knew it. The worst thing we could do was lose."

Coach Crowe found himself glumly looking for silver linings after the tourney had gone sour. One hopeful sign was that the Indianapolis school board had finally started a junior high basketball program.

One reason no Indianapolis school had ever won the state tournament was that the city's players began competing in organized games later than everyone else. By ninth grade, when Naptown's boys suited up for their first real games, players from other Indiana towns and cities had been competing in coached and refereed contests for at least three years. Crowe himself had played on a sixth-grade team back in Whiteland. Had he grown up in Indianapolis, it would have been at least another three years before he put on a uniform.

Early in 1952, Crowe began to hear about Flap Robertson's younger brother Oscar, an eighth grader at P.S. 17. According to Oscar's coach, Tom Sleet, the boy was the unquestioned leader of the team and by far the best young player in Indianapolis. Oscar Robertson, Sleet said, played the game at a different level than any other player he had coached.

Oscar Robertson was a good student from a tight-knit, deeply religious family. His mother, Mazell, wrote and performed gospel songs with her church choir. Smart but shy, Oscar knew the answers in class but was reluctant to raise his hand. Still, he was well known and well liked at school. His wide, dimpled smile could light up a room.

Tom Sleet had taught the boy the fundamentals of the game, such as how to pivot and how to pass. But with Oscar Robertson, Sleet found, you could teach more, as if you were coaching an adult player. And you only had to tell him once. "Oscar had uncommon discipline," Sleet recalled. "Uncommon ability. Uncommon pride. He was quiet, but he had great presence. You did not chasten Oscar in front of the others. You took him aside as privately as possible and told him what you wanted done. Then he would do it. And he practiced constantly. He would stay afterward and practice the one-handed shot and the pick-and-roll with his friend Bill Brown, and then he would go home and practice some more on his own."

In 1952, P.S. 17 reached the championship game of Indianapolis's

Public School 17, Indianapolis's first junior high champions, in Oscar Robertson's eighth-grade year. Oscar is eighth from the left, directly above tall trophy. (*Indianapolis Recorder*)

first junior high tournament. Ray Crowe drove to Tech High to see the contest and check out this boy Tom Sleet was so excited about. Greeting friends throughout the gym, Crowe took a seat and turned his attention to the young player. Oscar Robertson was a tall, lean, gangly boy with large, slightly protruding eyes and a quiet, almost private manner. During the game he controlled the basketball as if it were on a string attached to his fingers. He saw the entire court. He directed his teammates around the floor by pointing out spots for them to go, and he rewarded their obedience with feather-soft passes that allowed them to score easy baskets. It was as if the others were playing checkers and Oscar Robertson was playing chess. He never seemed to make a move unsupported by the logic of basketball.

At the end of each quarter Oscar bounced the ball patiently, crouching over it but looking up at the scoreboard clock until only a few seconds remained. Then he squared his body, paralyzed his defender with two or three quick fakes, and dropped the ball easily through the hoop just before the buzzer sounded. There was an element of contempt in his total control of those final seconds.

Here, thought Ray Crowe, was hope. "He just ran the game," Crowe later remembered, still smiling. "I had never seen any kid like that."

ROSENBERG SPIES EXECUTED
HALLIE BRYANT THREATENED

All-Star Ace Defies Bet-Fixer

By JEP CADOU JR.
Star Sports Editor

A vicious threat of physical injury late yesterday failed to scare Hallie Bryant out of playing in tonight's Indiana-Kentucky All-Star game.

The big Crispus Attucks

Die In Chair As Red Spies

JULIUS ROSENBERG   ETHEL ROSENBERG

Deaths End Years' Long Legal Fight

By BOB CONSIDINE

Sing Sing Prison, N. Y. (INS) — Julius and Ethel Rosenberg, the atomic spies who committed the "crime worse than murder," paid in full measure for it last night in the seething electric chair at Sing Sing.

Attucks's star players were household names in Indiana. Here the *Indianapolis Star* gave equal billing to a death threat against Hallie Bryant and the 1953 execution of Julius and Ethel Rosenberg, convicted as Soviet spies. (*Indianapolis Star/USA TODAY* Network)

Ten for the Referees

Shelbyville ended any illusions I had that it would be easy . . . but I had faith.
All we needed were players good enough to take the
officials out of the game.

—Ray Crowe

Senior **Willie Gardner rose when** the bell rang, ending history class, and started for the door. His teacher, Mr. Southern, came to his side and asked him to stick around a minute. "No, you're not in trouble," Mr. Southern said. "I just want you to know something before you read the papers." Gardner, the best player in Indiana, had just been declared ineligible for the 1952—53 basketball season by the Indiana High School Athletic Association.

The reason, the IHSAA explained, was that Willie had used up all three years of his eligibility to play competitive sports. The records showed that he had put on an Attucks uniform and sat on the varsity bench one game during his freshman year. It didn't matter that he hadn't played in the game. He had used up one of his three years simply by appearing once in a uniform. The rules were clear, and, once again, the penalties brutally severe. There would be no senior basketball season for Willie Gardner.

Ray Crowe had been pointing to 1953 as the year Attucks would at last win the tournament. Willie Gardner, Hallie Bryant, and Flap Robertson would all be seniors. With a veteran core of great players, Attucks would be unbeatable. But now, because of a petty rule that was rarely if ever enforced, the state's best player—a six-eight center as agile and quick as a guard—had been snatched away. Over the past two years, Gardner had averaged nearly 20 points per game. It was an understatement to say he was irreplaceable. When he heard the news, Willie Gardner asked Coach Crowe if he could be student manager.

With Gardner not playing, Attucks lost two of their first four games. Then they gelled, losing again only once in nineteen games before the tourney. By the season's end, Hallie Bryant had set a city scoring record. He and Flap Robertson both were named to the Indiana all-star team, composed of the ten best players in Indiana. Bryant was voted "Mr. Basketball," the best of the best. Early in the season, the mammoth crowds had begun to build again.

Alonzo Watford's office phone was now constantly busy. The callers were athletic directors, many from Indiana's most prominent high schools, white men who were practically begging for a chance to play Crispus Attucks at Butler Fieldhouse. The reason was simple: money. Butler University's contract with Attucks stipulated that whenever two Indianapolis high schools played in Butler Fieldhouse, ticket revenues were to be split evenly between the two schools. Since Attucks brought in thousands of fans, a single game at Butler against the Tigers could pay for an opponent's new uniforms, freshly painted bleachers, and maybe even a raise for the coach. "One game with us could make their whole year," Watford later said with a laugh.

Soon Alonzo Watford's Attucks Athletic Fund contained $25,000, enough to buy equipment for Attucks's shop and tailoring classes. The school got a new printing press. Watford bought several sets of uniforms for the varsity squad, including both dress whites and home green-and-golds. Their new warm-up jerseys came with capes bearing the imprinted images of snarling tigers. The Tigers were still vagabonds, going from gym to gym without a home court of their own, but now they traveled around Indiana in stylish double-decker buses. The rising fortune lifted all athletic teams at Attucks: Watford bought the track team a full set of hurdles—they had only had two—so that Attucks could at last host track meets. Now they were able to field a tennis team and a wrestling team. The baseball team got new uniforms.

And because of the surging crowds that followed them everywhere, Attucks was finally able to schedule games against the more competitive schools they needed to play to produce champions. Everyone wanted a cut of that money, especially at the fifteen thousand—seat Butler Fieldhouse. After begging for a chance to play for so many years, after being broke and homeless for decades, the team had gone from rags to riches. Suddenly marquee games and small fortunes were falling into Alonzo Watford's lap. "It got so I could play Podunk and make money," Watford later recalled, the memory filling his eyes with tears. "Man, what a feeling!"

Around this time, an African American man named Bernard McPeak applied for membership in the Indiana Officials Association, a statewide professional organization of high school basketball referees. McPeak hoped to become Indiana's first black referee, and he thought he was surpassingly well qualified. He had refereed for fifteen years in his home state of Pennsylvania, officiating four state championship games. He was respected as one of Pennsylvania's top referees. But he was rejected in Indiana by a vote of 40—7. The organization's president, Clayton Nichols, matter-of-factly explained the reason to a reporter: "It was because of his color."

Officiating had bedeviled Attucks year after year. The Tigers never saw a black referee. "When Attucks started going good, some of those [referees] were absolute bigots," recalled Bob Collins, then a sports columnist for the *Indianapolis Star*. "When there was a minute left to play in a close game, once that black hand came around that white hand to slap the ball away, that whistle would blow."

Some of the referees' calls were downright comical. Attucks played a game against Lafayette Jefferson High in which referees called five fouls against Willie Gardner in the first eight minutes of the game, disqualifying him from further play. Dejected, Gardner walked to the bench and sat down. Moments later, there was a scuffle under the basket and a referee whistled yet another foul on "number thirteen." Gardner raised his hand from the bench. "I guess they just wanted to make sure," he quipped.

Ray Crowe, a practical man, disciplined himself not to yell at referees. He remained in his seat during the games, grinding his teeth and popping his jaws. He told his bench players to stay seated and let him do the talking. But after his first year, the Tigers' coach realized that he had to factor bigotry into his game plan. Too many close calls went against Attucks to leave the game in doubt. He told his players that they simply had to get off to a fast start and build a big lead, for if the score was close at the end, the referees would be able to take the victory away from them. Before each game the Attucks coaches and players would join hands, look into one another's eyes, and say in unison, "The first ten points are for the refs. The rest are for us."

The most damaging call of all ended the 1952—53 season and dashed Attucks's tournament hopes yet again. After the loss of Willie Gardner, Crowe had pieced the team back together and had plowed through a twenty-six-game schedule with only three losses. Then the Tigers won the first two rounds of the tourney and were clear favorites to win the third, or semi-final, round, which would have put them into the state finals. Black Indianapolis—and increasingly all of Indianapolis—saw this team as the best chance the city had ever had to win a state championship.

Attucks's opponent, Shelbyville High School, used a predictable strategy. Knowing they could not outrun the Tigers, Shelbyville's Golden Bears slowed the game down, tossing the ball back and forth, trying to keep the score close to the very end and hoping for a break. The strategy worked to perfection. With fifty-eight seconds remaining and the score tied at 44, Attucks gave the ball to Hallie Bryant and organized its offense for a final shot. As the clock wound down, Hallie spotted an opening in the defense and broke for the Attucks basket, dribbling the ball furiously. When he left his feet, he was wide open for the shot, but two Shelbyville players quickly converged on him—one from each side—and knocked him to the floor. The three players went down in a tangle.

When he looked up, Hallie Bryant saw referee Stan Dubis's finger pointing at him. Dubis was claiming that Bryant had charged into one of the Shelbyville players. He gave the ball to Shelbyville's Jim Plymate, who hit the two free throws that ended yet another Attucks season.

The reaction was disbelief. The *Star*'s Bob Collins recalled later, "Charles Preston, a writer from the *Indianapolis Recorder*, and I went

The *Recorder*'s coverage of the referee scandal was front-page news in March 1953. (*Indianapolis Recorder*)

Negro Referee Barred
'Because of His Color'

By CHARLES S. PRESTON

The Indiana Officials Association—organization of the supposedly impartial, fair-minded referees who call the tune in high school basketball tournaments and other games— last week refused membership to a qualified official because he is a Negro.

How do you like that!

The group's fanatically prejudiced stand was taken only a few days before Attucks' Tigers were ousted from the tournament on a last-minute decision that many thousands of fans couldn't stomach.

The Association's biased action was revealed to The Recorder by none other than its president, Clayton Nichols.

Bitterly assailing his fellow-arbiters for their anti-Negro stand, Nichols said he believes firmly in democracy but was powerless to sway the organization.

STORY OF THE 'DISPUTED CALL' ON HALLIE BRYANT ON PAGES 11, 16

The rejected applicant is Bernard McPeak, veteran official of some 15 years' experience, who has refereed four state final playoffs in Pennsylvania, where he formerly lived.

McPeak is certified by the Indiana High School Athletic Association (IHSAA) and has worked a number of high school games here. His latest assignment was the Attucks-Ladoga contest at Tech's gym on Feb. 21

Members Discuss Rules

A POSTAL WORKER IN PRIVATE LIFE, Mr. McPeak told The Recorder his story last week.

He said that like anyone active in a particular field, he became interested in the officials' group with the idea that he might rub elbows with his fellows, compare note on "trade matters," and otherwise profit by the advantages of cooperation.

The Indiana Officials Association, as described by Mr. Nichols, resembles a professional group like a Press Club for newspaper workers. The members meet once a week, discuss rules and interpretations and the fine points of handling games.

It is also "a kind of clearing-house," and has published a directory for use of high schools and other game promoters in selecting officials.

The association has no connection with the IHSAA. However, since it is "the" organization of referees, it is bound to wield considerable influence.

Despite its title, the Association's membership is confined to Central Indiana—Indianapolis, Shelbyville, Anderson, Franklin and other nearby towns. It has 218 members. There are similar organizations in other districts of the state.

Demands Vote Recorded

McPEAK SAID HE ASKED FOR AN APPLICATION CARD, but never received one. Instead, in a few days he was informed by Nichols that his application had been rejected. Apparently all the members needed to know about him was one fact—his race.

"Is it true that your organization has turned down the application of Bernard McPeak?" The Recorder asked Nichols.

"Yes, that's true, as I explained to Mac," he replied.

"For what reason was he turned down?"

Without hesitation the president said:

"Because of his color."

Nichols then explained that he personally had supported the candidacy of the Negro official, along with a handful of others who believe in fair play regardless of race.

"But when it came to a vote there were only 7 of us for him and 40-some against.

"I demanded that my vote be recorded as favoring McPeak's admission. So did Ott Hurrle. That was done." (Hurrle is a former Butler athlete and popular young official.)

Nichols said his term as president is about over. Election of new officers will be held next Monday.

2nd-Class Sportsmanship?

THE RECORDER TALKED WITH ANOTHER OFFICIAL whom we have regarded as one of the fairest in town. He said that although a member of the Association, he had not been present at the meeting and knew nothing of the issue.

However, he added that he is doubtful whether Negroes should serve as officials, because "the crowd would be against them."

We do not believe this man realizes that he is laboring under the idea of second-class citizenship for Negroes on the basketball floor. Still, we would not like to trust his judgment on a split-second decision in a roaring Fieldhouse.

Still less do we like to trust hairline calls in the great game of basketball to officials who have shown, by a 40-to-7 vote, that they don't have the elementary democracy and decency of school children.

If that is what they do to a man, what do they do to the boys?

into the referees' dressing room and found Dubis after the game. We said, 'Are you sure that was charging?' 'Absolutely,' he said. We asked again and he looked away. No way he believed that."

The following Saturday the *Recorder*'s Charles Preston held nothing back in a blistering editorial: "Some have called umpire Stan Dubis's decision 'questionable,' but in the mind of this writer and countless others there was no question about it. It was wrong, raw and inexcusable."

Hallie Bryant took it hardest of all. "I can't think of anything else," he told a reporter days later. "It was the awfulest thing that ever happened to me. I didn't foul anybody. I guess this will be with me the rest of my life."

"After that Shelbyville game," Ray Crowe later said, "I began to realize how difficult it was going to be to win a championship. I was discouraged, but I wasn't about to give up. I told myself that if we continued to work hard and do our best, eventually we'd come through and win it all. What else could I think?"

In his *Recorder* editorial, Preston summed up the 1952—53 Attucks season with a question that must have been on Ray Crowe's mind as well, no matter how much he detested excuses. Preston wrote: "Many Negro young people, and others who are trying to believe in a democratic America, were asking this week: 'Is it always going to be true that officials will take the close games away from Attucks, the close fights away from Negro boxers? Has a person with a dark skin got a chance for fair play?'"

Attucks cheering section at Butler Fieldhouse. (Courtesy Crispus Attucks Museum)

"To Be Around My People"

I loved my time at Attucks . . . Aside from on the basketball court,
there was no place I would rather have been. It sounds corny, but sitting in class,
having teachers who you knew cared—cared not just about me as a player,
but as a person—that made me feel good. Special.

—Oscar Robertson, *The Big O*

Each summer on the day after school let out, Bailey, Henry, and Oscar Robertson boarded a Greyhound bus at the Illinois Street terminal and headed south to spend the summer at their grandparents' farm in Tennessee. They were eagerly awaited. "Eight hours and three hundred miles later, my grandmother would be crushing us in her bosom with massive hugs," Oscar wrote.

Most days were spent in the field, planting and plowing. When the sun was straight overhead, their grandfather would look up and declare it time for lunch. They'd sit under a tree and open the brown sacks their grandmother had packed with chicken and greens and pound cake. Then in the long, slow evenings after dinner, their grandfather would recite from memory beautiful passages from the Bible. Sometimes he would break into his favorite song, "Old Time Religion," and everyone would sing. They were magical summers.

After three months of country food and outdoor work, the Robertson boys always returned to Indiana a little bigger and stronger than when they left. But what happened to Oscar Robertson in the summer of his fourteenth year was the stuff of fable. When he got on the bus bound for the farm at the end of his freshman year at Attucks, he stood about five-eight. Three months later, when the bus door opened in Indianapolis, the Oscar Robertson who stepped out stood nearly six feet four, with the powerful arms and shoulders of a working man. A summer of outdoor toil combined with a miracle of puberty had put nearly seven inches on him. His arms were ribbons of sinewy muscle, his shoulders wide, his chest thick and broad.

His friends were astonished.

In the final weeks of the summer of 1953, Oscar went about settling some old scores at Lockefield Gardens. Now the players who had leaned on him and pushed him out of the way just a summer earlier found themselves overmatched and outmuscled. Those people included Flap. "For years I had been able to beat him," Flap recalled. "I would give him points, to even out my advantage. Then all of a sudden the trend reversed. It was so sudden. Now he was two inches taller than me. And *strong*. And then people started choosing him at Lockefield before me. He could do whatever he wanted to do."

Oscar also began to win the one-on-one games he played with Hallie Bryant. "When I could sense that he could beat me, I stopped playing him so it wouldn't happen," Bryant remembered. "I struggled

with it. But I learned to grit my teeth and pull for him. I had to wipe out the jealous feelings I had."

Back in June, before he left for Tennessee, Oscar had had to wait in line at courtside with boys his age, hoping to be noticed and trying to get into a game, threatening to take his ball home if he couldn't play. No more. Now, in September 1953 and for the rest of his life, Oscar Robertson was an asset to any team.

· · ·

Ray Crowe had to start over with the 1953—54 Attucks team. The first wave of Frog Islanders educated in his after-school intramural program was gone now. Hallie Bryant had won a full scholarship to play basketball for Indiana University. Flap Robertson had won a scholarship to play on the Indiana Central College squad. And something even better had happened to Willie Gardner. On a sportswriter's dare, Gardner, now nineteen, had traveled with his Attucks teammate Cleveland Harp to Chicago to take part in a massive public tryout for the Harlem Globetrotters. Over five hundred African American players had gathered from around the nation, hoping to land a spot among the lucky few who traveled the world playing basketball and entertaining countless fans.

The Globetrotters had the nation's best African American players of the day. At that time there were only three black players in the National Basketball Association, with no certain prospects that there would ever be more. The Globetrotter tryout attracted players who had earned big reputations on college teams. Willie Gardner, having played only through his junior year in high school, was completely unknown.

First, there were ball-handling drills. Gardner, now six-nine and starting to fill out, could complete sharp passes without even looking at the target. In fact, no big man at the tryout controlled the ball as well as he did that day. "Can anybody here dunk the ball?" the workout leader asked. Gardner raised his hand, then did his Attucks pregame routine—left-hand dunk, right-hand dunk, and two-handed over the head—but for the Globetrotter tryout, he added a new touch: he ran toward the hoop carrying a ball in each huge hand, leaped high above the rim, and slammed them down, one after the other.

Marques Haynes, one of the Globetrotters' established stars, walked over to the team's owner, Abe Saperstein, who was watching from the sidelines. "Where'd you find that boy?" Haynes asked.

Saperstein himself was wondering where the kid had come from, but he took credit. "Pure genius," he replied.

That afternoon, Willie Gardner signed a Globetrotter contract, sending the money back home to his mother. He reported to Globetrotter rookie camp the next morning. Cleveland Harp, the second Attucks star at the tryout, remembered it well. "There were thirty-three rookies in camp," Harp recalled. "Thirty-one college players and us. Rookies practiced on one court . . . veterans on another. Willie practiced only one day with the rookies. The next day they put him with the main team. He was probably the best ballplayer in the country in 1953." Harp himself made a Globetrotter traveling squad. Willie Gardner spent his next three and a half years traveling around the world to the delight of millions, doing what he loved to do most.

Oscar Robertson, now fourteen years old and entering his sophomore year of high school, practiced with intense focus in the weeks before the tryout for the 1953—54 Attucks team. He would have to be at his best, for sophomores almost never made the Attucks varsity. When tryout day came, nearly eighty boys showed up. Crowe and his assistants, Al Spurlock and Tom Sleet, divided the players into two groups and told them to sit down. Group one consisted of thirty to forty older players, juniors and seniors trying out for the Attucks varsity team. Group two was mainly sophomores hoping to make the junior varsity team. Oscar shyly sat down with the younger group.

But Bill Mason, a senior and an established Attucks player whom Oscar knew from the outdoor courts, beckoned to Oscar with his crooked finger. "Come over here," Bill said. Oscar looked around, then took a chance. He stood, walked to the varsity side, and sat down among the older players. Crowe put Oscar with a group of second stringers and matched them against the varsity starters in a series of hotly contested games. The tryout might have intimidated another young player, but Oscar had been playing against the varsity guys at Lockefield for years. He gave it everything he had.

When the Razor made his final cut, Oscar Robertson's name was on the varsity squad. Carrying on Flap's tradition, he was now a Crispus Attucks Tiger.

"I walked home in a daze," Oscar later wrote, "and about burst with pride when I told Bill Swatts, my friend."

Though the team was young, Crowe had great talent to work with on the 1953–54 Attucks squad. One of the best players was junior Willie Merriweather, as tall as Oscar and an even better leaper. Unlike most of the other Attucks players, Merriweather *chose* to attend Attucks. He could have gone to Shortridge High, a predominantly white school on the city's near-northside, or he could have gone to Attucks—the black school.

In 1949, Indianapolis had adopted a "neighborhood" school policy, dividing the city into school districts and mandating that students attend schools within the district where they lived. However, two giant loopholes made the scheme all but meaningless: First, the few white students who lived in Frog Island were granted "vouchers" to transfer to a school outside their neighborhood if they did not wish to attend Attucks; all took the transfer. Second, black students in Indianapolis who did not live within the Attucks district were allowed to "cross the line" and go to Attucks instead of attending their neighborhood school; most went to Attucks.

The arrangement set off a wild scramble by city high school coaches for talented black basketball players who lived outside the

Attucks district. The year before, Mazell Robertson, now divorced from Bailey Sr. and working two jobs, had purchased a home big enough for Oscar and Henry to have their own bedrooms. The house happened to be just within the Shortridge school district. Shortridge athletic officials instantly claimed Oscar and Henry as their own, but the boys insisted on staying at Attucks. At one point the discussion became so heated that Mazell simply threatened to move back to Colter Street if the Shortridge officials didn't leave her sons alone. "My sons are not for sale," she informed the world.

Willie Merriweather's parents had likewise scraped together enough money to purchase a home just north of the Attucks school district. Willie had gone to nearly all-white elementary and junior high schools within the Shortridge district and expected to attend Shortridge High School. In fact, he had actually enrolled at Shortridge in the fall of 1953 and had already received his orientation package. Yet he could not get Oscar Robertson off his mind.

Like Ray Crowe, Willie Merriweather had been in the Tech bleachers the day Oscar led his team to the Indianapolis eighth-grade championship in 1952. Merriweather was captivated. There was something about Oscar—the way he carried himself, his obvious pride in his school, his leadership as a player—that struck a chord with Merriweather. "Meeting him, seeing him win that championship . . . I just had a yearning to be around my people," he later explained. At the last instant, Merriweather withdrew from Shortridge and enrolled at Attucks, a move he never regretted.

The other new additions to Ray Crowe's 1953–54 team were center Sheddrick Mitchell, a tall, introverted boy from Mississippi with a gorgeous hook shot, and two young guards, Bill Hampton and Bill Scott. Both were smart ball handlers and tenacious defenders. Bill Brown, Oscar's longtime friend, also made the squad. Like Oscar, Brown didn't say much but made himself heard through his game. He was a tremendous rebounder, often leaping high and ripping the ball out of the air with both hands, elbows flying and legs out. Bodies seemed to shower off Bill Brown.

As always, Ray Crowe's new players were remarkably poor. Many of their mothers worked as domestics, taking in ironing and washing or working in the homes of white women. Some of them worked at two or three jobs. Elonora Merriweather—Willie's mom—got by on $96 a month in Social Security benefits and $19 a week from the white woman for whom she worked as a cook.

Bill Scott's situation was probably grimmest of all. When Bill was twelve, the family had moved to Indianapolis from a small Alabama coal town that had dried up suddenly. Bill's father had long before disappeared from Bill's life, and his mother had given the boy to his grandmother to raise. After a while his mother, too, went to Indianapolis to stay with a sister. Two weeks after Bill arrived in Indianapolis, his mother was pulled from a streetcar, dragged into an alley, raped, and murdered. When Ray Crowe came to know him, Bill Scott lived in half of a converted garage a few blocks from Indiana Avenue with his grandmother and an uncle who drank heavily. Bill Scott saw basketball on the Attucks team as a way out of that garage.

Oscar Robertson's career on the Attucks varsity basketball team got off to a shaky start. Attucks's first game, against Fort Wayne North Side, was to be played at Arsenal Technical High's east-side Indianapolis gym. Oscar decided to take a bus across town to get to the game. But the vehicle crawled through the city blocks, stopping at almost every corner as game time approached. On top of that, a deranged passenger brandished a knife at Oscar, causing him to back off the bus and start walking east toward Tech as fast as he could.

Oscar made it to the gym but began the game on the bench,

wearing Flap's old number 43 on his green-and-gold jersey. Ray Crowe waited all of three minutes to put him in the game. He started every game after that for the next three years. Oscar scored fifteen points and Attucks won easily. The *Indianapolis Star*, eyebrow raised, praised Oscar for "poise unexpected of a sophomore."

An even stronger hint of Oscar Robertson's presence came in a December game between Attucks and Indianapolis Shortridge for the city championship. Playing before nearly nine thousand fans in Butler Fieldhouse, Attucks fell behind 22–9 in the first quarter and seemed overmatched. In fact, they were stuffed. Earlier in the day, Ray Crowe had dropped the team off to eat lunch at the Indiana University Medical Center and left them alone while he went out to run some errands. When he came back, he found that they had helped themselves to seconds, then thirds, and that his bill was nearly $60 over budget.

At the beginning of the second quarter, Oscar, clearly disgusted with the Tigers' sluggish play, began to clap his hands and *demand* the ball. His teammates were startled.

"When he got the ball, he waved everybody aside," remembered teammate John Gipson. "He took over offensively all the time, but just to wave everybody off—that was the first time we'd seen that." They gave it to Oscar, and he hit shot after shot. When defenders inched forward to stop him from shooting, he faked and drove past them to the basket. With a minute left, Oscar hit a layup that put Attucks ahead for the first time, but Shortridge tied the game and sent it into overtime. After Attucks fell behind, Oscar stole the ball and drove again to send the game into a second overtime, which he won with a jump shot.

The Shortridge game caused two changes. Before, newspaper reporters had referred to Oscar as "Little Flap" Robertson. After that, he was just "Oscar."

And never again would Ray Crowe let his players gorge themselves just before a game.

On December 8, 1953, a week before the first Attucks—Tech matchup of the season, a white Tech reserve guard named David Huff was walking home from basketball practice, lost in thought, when three black men sprang from a parked car and blocked his way. One grabbed Huff's collar and drew him near while the other two pulled knives.

"You're Huff," said the group's spokesman.

The boy nodded, dry mouthed.

"You're a good shot, but you better not play too good [against Attucks]. If you make one single point . . . we'll come back and cut you open." And they let him go.

Oscar Robertson dueling with an opponent. (*Indianapolis Star/ USA TODAY* Network)

Arsenal Technical High School was the largest school in the state of Indiana, with an enrollment exceeding five thousand students. Tech and Attucks were natural rivals: Tech was on the east side of Indianapolis, Attucks on the west. Attucks was all black, Tech nearly all white, although this year there were two black players on the varsity basketball squad.

Huff reported the incident to police, and it was all over the next day's newspapers. Canceling the game was discussed. More anonymous threats followed. Notes scrawled in pencil on toilet paper arrived at Huff's home and that of his coach. "Keep Huff and [Don] Sexton out of the ball game," one read. "We mean it." Death threats against Attucks players Winfred O'Neal and Bill Mason reached Attucks school officials. One author showed his hand a bit, writing, "I have all my possessions bet on the game, including my car and house, and I want to see Tech win." The phone rang at the Robertson house, too. Oscar took the call. "If I played, the guy said, he was going to shoot me," Oscar remembered. "I told him to go to hell."

Brown v. Board of Education of Topeka

In the winter of 1953, as the Tigers took on a tough city schedule, the United States Supreme Court decided to take a fresh look at whether racially segregated public schools such as Attucks were legal under the U.S. Constitution. The question had been simmering for a long time. In 1896, in a famous court case known as *Plessy v. Ferguson*, the U.S. Supreme Court had ruled that the State of Louisiana could racially segregate its buses, streetcars, and trains without violating the U.S. Constitution as long as the separate sections of compartments were "equal."

"Separate but equal" became the legal basis for segregation in public schools. But the claim that schools built for blacks and whites were "equal" was a sham. In 1900, $15.41 was spent on each white child in the public schools versus $1.50 per black student. The ratio was the same forty years later.

It was the notion of separate but equal that the Supreme Court struck down in *Brown v. Topeka Board of Education* in 1954. Shortly after noon on Monday, May 17, 1954, Earl Warren, chief justice of the United States, began to read from an eleven-page opinion: "We unanimously conclude that in the field of public education the doctrine of 'separate but equal' has no place." The landmark decision outlawed segregated schools as a violation of the Fourteenth Amendment's "equal protection" clause. Observers predicted that the ruling would soon change the lives of twelve million schoolchildren in the seventeen southern and border states and the four northern states—including Indiana—that permitted segregated schools.

The court's decision did not set a deadline for compliance. Integration would take place with "all deliberate speed." While IMPEACH EARL WARREN billboards sprouted like weeds along Indiana roadways, Hoosier communities moved at a snail's pace to integrate their classrooms. It would take seventeen years and another court order before the first white student attended Crispus Attucks High.

Security was tight at Butler Fieldhouse for the Attucks–Tech game. Along with more than ten thousand fans, there were dozens of plain-clothes police officers combing the stands for potential problems. David Huff was kept from playing in the game by his parents and coach. The decision brought him to tears. Cops patrolled both dressing rooms and followed the teams out on the floor for warm-up drills. The game itself was poorly played by two squads of jittery, emotionally drained teens. Attucks took an early lead, stretched it to 14 points, and then held on to win 43–38. It is safe to say that many dollars changed hands.

Attucks approached the 1954 tournament with barely half a team. The frontcourt had been demolished. Willie Merriweather, Winfred O'Neal, and Sheddrick Mitchell had all sustained season-ending injuries. "Attucks's Long Reign of Supremacy Is Over," headlined the *Indianapolis News* in a pre-tournament roundup.

Out of a mixture of panic and pragmatism, Ray Crowe put a new wrinkle into his game plan, an innovation that would affect the very future of basketball.

He put Oscar Robertson in the backcourt. This seemed to run against all common sense and historical wisdom. The second-tallest player on the team, Oscar was a powerful rebounder and a brilliant scorer close to the basket. Why move him farther away? The answer was that Robertson was also the team's best ball handler and leader. He saw the entire court and seemed to know what was going to happen before it actually did, often because he forced the action himself. It made sense to put the ball in his hands as much as possible.

"Oscar's will was evident from the beginning," Ray Crowe reflected later. "It's just something that he had that the others didn't have. It's hard to put your finger on what makes a champion. But Oscar was a great example." Letting Oscar bring the ball up court put him in a quarterback's position, allowing him to see how the defense was deployed against Attucks and to adjust. Also, the strategy put Oscar's hand on the throttle to activate the fast break, which was Attucks's preferred style of attack.

With Oscar at the helm, Attucks picked up momentum and finished the season 17—4. The Tigers cruised through the sectional and regional rounds of the state tournament, and easily defeated their first two opponents in the Indianapolis semi-final round.

For the chance to advance to the final four, Attucks had to defeat Milan High, a tiny southeastern Indiana school with only 161 students enrolled, merely 73 of them boys. Like many other small Indiana schools, Milan boasted a gym that could seat the population of the entire town. But the Milan team was not just another batch of farm boys with delusions of tournament victory. Though small, Milan was a smartly coached squad of talented players, some of whom had been playing on teams together since third grade. Over the years, they had developed an almost mystical sense of each other on a basketball court. Like Attucks, they had a historic mission: They were determined to become the first truly small school ever to win the

Indiana state tournament. Indiana was one of only three states that did not divide its postseason basketball tournament into classes by enrollment size. Everyone played everyone else in Indiana, meaning little crossroads schools often faced off against big-city teams. Unfair as it seemed, the format fit the Hoosier philosophy: in Indiana everyone got a chance, but no one a handout.

Hoosiers being filmed in an Indiana Catholic school gym. (Frank Fisse/*Indianapolis Star*/*USA TODAY* Network)

Hoosiers, the Hollywood Film

Released in 1986, *Hoosiers* is one of the most successful sports movies of all time. It stars Gene Hackman, Barbara Hershey, and Dennis Hopper. The story is loosely based on the 1954 Indiana state high school championship game between tiny Milan High and huge Muncie Central High, a game won by Bobby Plump's buzzer-beating shot for Milan.

The filmmakers took plenty of liberties in celebrating Indiana's famous season-ending tournament. They renamed the schools (Milan became Hickory, Muncie became South Bend), gave the coach a haunted past and a romantic interest, and let the town drunk help coach a big game.

One invented portion raised the ire of Oscar Robertson and many other viewers. Robertson wrote in 2003: "What does it mean that the filmmakers twisted the truth? Instead of having Milan defeat Muncie Central and an integrated team with two black guys on it [actually, Muncie Central's team had three black players—John Casterlow, Jimmy Barnes, and Robert Crawford], which is what happened in real life, Hickory defeated a fictional team of black players, coached exclusively by black men . . . Is the proverbial race card being played?"

On March 13, 1954, Attucks met Milan in the semi-final round of the state tournament at Butler Fieldhouse in Indianapolis. Some Indianapolis fans found themselves torn about which team to root for. In the forty-three-year history of the Indiana tournament, no Indianapolis team had ever won. It was humiliating. Out-of-town relatives poked fun all summer long, every year. An Attucks victory could put an end to the snickering once and for all.

On the other hand, all the Attucks players were black and all of Milan's were white—that was still too much for some fans to deal with.

The Milan players spent the night before the game against Attucks in the Pennsylvania Hotel in downtown Indianapolis. Some Milan players had never been to Indianapolis before. Milan star Bobby Plump remembers being amazed by the local hostility to Crispus Attucks High. "When we went out to dinner that night," recalls Plump, "an unusual number of people followed us around. One of the frequent remarks we heard was 'C'mon, Milan, beat those niggers.' People were saying it everywhere."

Milan brought the season crashing down upon Attucks. Realizing that they could not win by running against Attucks's fast-break

Milan star Bobby Plump scores against Crispus Attucks High in the 1954 semi-final round of the tourney. Oscar Robertson watches, facing Plump. (Courtesy Bobby Plump)

offense, the Milan players slowed the game down, walking the ball to the midcourt line and probing the Attucks defense with deft passes. Milan hit 60 percent of their shots in the first half, seized a comfortable lead, and controlled the pace of the game in the second half.

Milan's 65—52 victory was the worst defeat a Ray Crowe—coached team had ever absorbed, or ever would again. Oscar Robertson scored 22 points, but it wasn't enough; Milan's unstoppable Plump had 28. And the following week, Milan lived out their dream, defeating Muncie Central—a team whose gym could seat seven times the entire population of Milan—on a game-ending last-second jump shot by Bobby Plump.

When Milan beat Attucks and, a week later, Muncie Central, the curtain came down forever on the farm-boy era of basketball in Indiana and, perhaps, in the United States. After the 1954 tourney, fourteen of the next seventeen Indiana high school champions came from big-city schools, many populated with African American players.

Like ships in the night, Attucks and Milan passed each other in 1954, one representing the urban future of basketball and the other its rural past.

And it would be, with one meaningless exception, nearly three years before anyone ever beat Crispus Attucks High again.

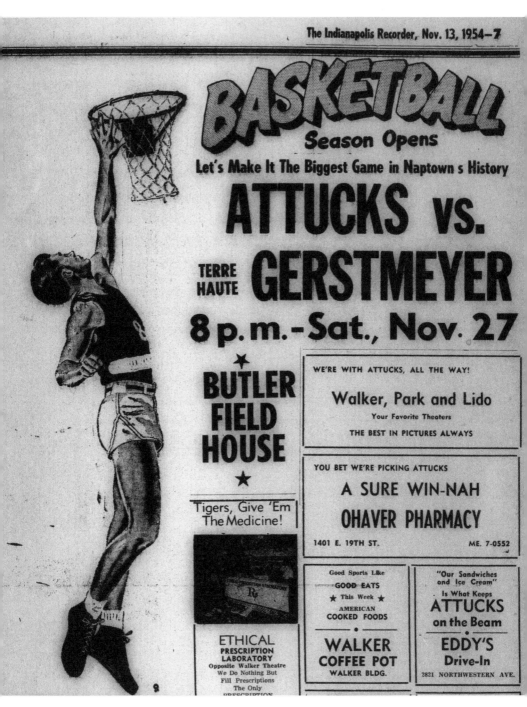

BASKETBALL
Season Opens

Let's Make It The Biggest Game in Naptown's History

ATTUCKS vs.

TERRE HAUTE **GERSTMEYER**

8 p.m. - Sat., Nov. 27

★
BUTLER FIELD HOUSE
★

Tigers, Give 'Em The Medicine!

Attucks's 1954–55 season began with a match against a tough team from Terre Haute. One by one, the little country schools were being replaced in Attucks's schedule by city powerhouses like Gerstmeyer. (*Indianapolis Recorder*)

"Attucks Was *Ours*"

Man, it was sweet. Smiles everywhere—everywhere. And tears, too.
Oh, yes, plenty of tears. I personally hugged two people I disliked
and every friend I could find. It was something.

—An Attucks fan

Hopes were high among Attucks fans in the autumn of 1954. Seventy-six boys tried out for the varsity, including several exceptionally talented players. Willie Merriweather, now a senior, was at last free of injury. Oscar Robertson, still only a fifteen-year-old junior, was named by some forecasters as the best player in the state.

The days of competing against backwoods schools were at last behind them; now Attucks would test themselves against nearly every top ten team in the state. Sportswriter Charles Preston puffed out his chest in his basketball preview for the *Indianapolis Recorder*: "Pardon us, fellas, if we jump the gun, but Ray Crowe has seven veterans back, Willie Merriweather has grown an inch and a half, Oscar Robertson is shooting goals all day long in an alley behind Cornelius Avenue—and away we go!"

Attucks stormed out of the gate, winning its first sixteen games in the winter of 1954, most by outlandish margins. By New Year's Day 1955, it had become clear to basketball fans in Indiana that if you wanted to see Attucks play, you'd better arrive early, because most of their games were over by halftime. It was also clear that this season Oscar Robertson and his Attucks teammates might be a once-in-a-lifetime team, maybe the best that Hoosiers had ever seen.

The idea was sobering for many—blacks and whites alike. America's attention had turned to race relations during that winter of 1954—55, largely driven by the U.S. Supreme Court ruling that the nation's public schools would eventually have to be racially integrated. Crispus Attucks students were studying black history without being fully aware that their basketball team was making it. In English and history courses, the team members and their classmates were reading and discussing classic black liberation works. "I pretty much went through the equivalent of a Black Studies program," Oscar Robertson later wrote, "reading [W. E. B.] DuBois, [Ralph] Ellison, and [Richard] Wright."

While conflict was intensifying throughout the South in those dawning days of the civil rights movement, Indianapolis was also going through growing pains, much of it driven by basketball. The Attucks team was the talk of the town. Behind closed doors, at the dinner table, underneath the hair dryer, on the factory line, in diners and schools and showrooms, and at construction sites, talk was about the all-black school poised to win the Indiana High School Basketball Tournament. Either you wanted Attucks to get cut down to size ("There'll be no living with them," wrote one reader to the *Indianapolis Recorder*), or you wanted Attucks to run the table for the capital city. There was no in-between. Remembering that city officials had deliberately squeezed nearly all the city's black athletes into a single school, some whites asked one another: *What have we done?*

Just as civil rights protesters were making headlines in Alabama and Mississippi, every Attucks victory stirred passions in Indianapolis. Ray Crowe and the boys on the 1954—55 Attucks varsity were becoming activists for racial justice by excelling at something that was dearly prized by whites.

Crowds increased game by game, pouring through turnstiles at Indiana's biggest venues. In the first twenty-one games of the season, Attucks played before an average crowd of 8,226 fans, easily outdrawing the college and professional teams that also used Butler Fieldhouse. Seven of Attucks's first thirteen games had to be moved to Butler to accommodate ticket demands. One Wednesday evening game against Shortridge High attracted 11,561 fans to Butler—a gathering that sent fans hiking toward empty seats in far reaches of the cavernous stadium. A local newspaper declared it possibly "a world's record crowd for a non-tournament high school game." Attucks's share of the gate receipts for that game alone was $3,200.

To Russell Lane and Alonzo Watford, to all the African Americans who had refused to view themselves as outcasts, and to Attucks's splendid teachers and dedicated parents, the 1954—55 team was the golden dividend of a twenty-eight-year investment. The whole community—pastors and legislators, musicians and beauticians, maids and merchants, and parents and fans—had held together from the Klan days forward, refusing to view themselves as inferior as they built an outstanding school.

Now black children in Indiana had heroes of their own, in this case Oscar Robertson (left) and Willie Merriweather (right). (*Indianapolis Recorder*)

By now there was tradition even in the uniforms the players wore. Oscar Robertson wore his brother's number 43. Hallie Bryant had personally bequeathed his legendary number 34 to Bill Hampton, instructing him, "When you graduate, you pass it on to a good man, just like I did."

All that was left to accomplish was a state championship. It wouldn't be easy, but now, in the brilliant 1954—55 team Ray Crowe had assembled, they believed they had the hammer to drive the spike home.

Indianapolis was slowly opening doors to the boys who wore green-and-gold letter jackets with a big A. They were social pollinators. "Everywhere I went on the street it was, 'Scotty, let me buy you a sandwich,'" recalls Bill Scott. The players were even getting to know a few whites, mainly sportswriters but also merchants who owned finance companies, pawnshops, clothing stores, and car dealerships along Indiana Avenue.

"We were special," Willie Merriweather recalls. "Everyone knew us. We were always in the papers. We carried ourselves as special. [During the tournament] our pictures were in the windows of [department stores]. Block's, Ayres, Harry Levins. People wanted to give us clothes, watches, TVs, anything. We could eat free at Doyles. Our haircuts were free."

Many of the stores on Indiana Avenue were owned by Jewish businesspeople. "We sort of modeled ourselves after the store owners," Bill Scott would later recall. "We would see [them] in their Cadillacs, their casual open collars and suits made of nice silks and mixed blends. They had their own businesses. You sort of trust people who are successful."

Harold Stolkin, the owner of Indiana Finance, a loan company, became so close to the team that, for reasons the players never fully understood, Ray Crowe invited him and his young son Mark to sit on the Attucks bench during home games. They wore green-and-gold beanies on their heads.

Stolkin identified deeply with the Attucks players. In his view they were all outcasts getting by on Frog Island. His father was a Jewish merchant who had come to Indianapolis from Philadelphia early in the century to open a restaurant. But like other Jews during the Klan years, the elder Stolkin had been forced to locate his business along Indiana Avenue. Later he started a finance company specializing in no-money-down car loans to black residents, then turned the business over to Harold in the 1940s. Though Harold Stolkin did not live in the neighborhood, he considered himself to be a Frog Islander at heart.

Stolkin found the Attucks players jobs in the summer, and sometimes took them to restaurants owned by his friends. "I remember once he took us to the Italian Village at Twenty-Second and Meridian," said Bill Scott. "When the pizza came, we opened the box and smelled those anchovies. We said, 'Man, what *are* these things?' Some of us couldn't eat them."

A Crispus Attucks basketball player had little trouble getting dates, though serious romance was cooled by Ray Crowe's strict nine o'clock curfew. A few players now had their driver's licenses and access to wheels. Willie Merriweather cruised in his late father's '51 Olds 98. Bill Scott had the wheel of an immaculate '35 Chevy with dark curtains in the rear window. The cars' radio dials were glued to WLAC in Nashville (whose clear-channel designation allowed it to be heard throughout the Midwest), where rhythm-and-blues disc jockeys delivered Ray Charles and the Platters and LaVern Baker, whose records could be mail-ordered from sponsor Randy's Record Shop. Players buzzed Eddie's Drive-In at Udell and West, Al Green's on the east side, and even the white-owned TeePee, whose managers would let the black players park and order food as long as they stayed in their cars.

Ray Crowe urged his players to talk with reporters after their games, but Oscar Robertson would linger in the dressing room, avoiding reporters and photographers until they left. This fostered ever more curiosity about Oscar, which became almost obsessive as the season progressed. For the first time, many white fans found themselves wanting personal information about a black Hoosier, wondering about his family, his grades, and his dreams and college plans. One fan letter with five signatures reached the *Indianapolis Times*. "We have read so much about Oscar, you know, the only secrets about him are what he has for breakfast and what his girlfriend's name is," they wrote. "Can you enlighten us?" Reporter Jimmie Angelopolous did his best: "Oscar doesn't have a steady girlfriend this year . . . I don't know what Oscar likes for breakfast but if you'd send him a pie he'd eat it."

There was a cockiness to the 1954—55 team that had not been there even in the breakthrough days of Hallie Bryant and Willie Gardner. At times, Crowe had to get tough to maintain control. During one practice, Oscar berated a substitute who had muffed a pass that caused his team to lose an intrasquad game. Players fell silent as Ray Crowe walked slowly to his star. The moment remained vivid years later to Willie Merriweather: "Mr. Crowe walked over to Oscar and said, 'I am the coach of this team. Nobody will get on a player except me. You understand?' Oscar said yes, and then when Mr. Crowe went away, he mumbled something. Mr. Crowe grabbed him and turned him and smacked him. Told him to go down and take a shower. Oscar was kind of sniffling. We all looked at each other. We said, 'Shoot, if he'd hit Oscar, he'd *kill* us.' Nobody messed with Mr. Crowe . . . When practice was over, we went down in the locker room and asked Oscar, 'Are you gonna transfer to Shortridge?' Everyone was nervous that night, even Mr. Crowe."

Late in January, the team, undefeated and barely tested after sixteen games, played at Connersville High, a school about seventy miles southeast of Indianapolis. Connersville was one of the few small-town schools remaining on the schedule from the old days when city schools wouldn't compete against Attucks. Though the Attucks players took the contest lightly, it was the game of the year for Connersville. Thousands packed the tiny gym. Officials seated the overflow crowd in the school auditorium and broadcast the game over the public address system. Many whites generously gave up their seats in the gym to their African American guests who had made the drive from Indy to cheer on their Tigers. Officials roped off the court, seating even more spectators along the margin.

By halftime, Connersville, slowing the game to a crawl and holding the ball for minutes at a time, led 24—21. During the intermission, officials threw open the gym's doors to ventilate the stuffy room with fresh winter air. When play resumed, a thin veneer of ice coated the removable gym floor, which had been laid over a swimming pool. Connersville continued to play keepaway, using up time while Attucks players slipped and flailed in their increasingly desperate attempts to capture the ball. By the end of the third quarter, Connersville had built a 10-point lead. Attucks charged back, but Connersville held on to win by a single point.

There was deep silence on the bus ride home. The Tigers were no longer undefeated, and they would no longer be ranked first in the state. The players studied the back of Ray Crowe's head and saw his bulging jaws working in and out, and knew there would be a steep price to pay. The first installment came the next day—a brutal, nonstop, five-hour-long practice that left everyone exhausted. When it was finished, Crowe assembled the varsity and reserve squads before him on the bleacher seats. "From now on," he said, addressing the varsity, "no the one has a guaranteed spot on this team. You will have to earn your position every single game."

No team again came closer than 14 points that season until March, when Attucks played against Muncie Central in the championship game of the Indiana tournament's third round—the Indianapolis semi-final—at Butler Fieldhouse. The Attucks—Muncie Central game had the electric feel of a great heavyweight boxing match. All season long, the two teams had traded the number-one and number-two ranking positions in newspaper polls. Each team had lost only once. The *Star* called their showdown "the Game of the Century." For many, Muncie Central, probably the only team in Indiana capable of beating Attucks, was the white hope.

It was a game over which a great deal of money changed hands— black dollars and white dollars. Attucks games had long been heavily wagered, with racial prejudice driving many white fans to bet with their hearts rather than their heads against a black team. In the days before the Muncie game, long lines of cars formed at the Cities Service gas station at Sixteenth and Senate Avenue, a hub of basketball betting. Paychecks, automobile titles, and even home mortgages were wagered in the Chrysler and Allison Transmission factories of Indianapolis, and major sums were staked in "pea shake houses," named for a local gambling game, along Indiana Avenue.

The Crispus Attucks—Muncie Central game on March 12, 1955, played at a packed Butler Fieldhouse, was everything a fan could have hoped for. Attucks started fast, hitting four of its first five shots and taking an 18—9 lead by the end of the first quarter. Muncie fought back and took the lead by a single point at the quarter break. The lead changed fourteen times within the next sixteen minutes as tension built. Muncie's biggest problem was Oscar Robertson. They assigned their best defensive player, Gene Flowers, to stop him, but Oscar faked again and again, causing Flowers to lose his balance and then grab at Oscar as he drove past. Flowers was whistled for four fouls and spent much of the second half on the Muncie bench.

Attucks clung to a 6-point lead with little more than a minute to go when Willie Merriweather fouled out of the game, giving Muncie fresh hope. Muncie's aggressive pressure trapped Attucks guard Bill Hampton in the corner. Rather than passing the ball to a teammate, Hampton kept it, dribbling lower and lower as two Muncie players hemmed him in. Finally, Hampton ran out of space and the ball rolled out of bounds. Bill Scott remembers hearing one livid fan, probably with considerable money riding on Attucks, scream at Hampton after the turnover, "Man, why did you *do* that? I should *kill* you!" Muncie stole the ball again, scoring another field goal and a free throw. Muncie called a time-out with eleven seconds remaining, behind 71—70 but in possession of the ball.

The game, the season, and a quarter century's step-by-step progress at Attucks now hung on the next eleven seconds. The referee blew his whistle and handed the ball to Muncie's Gene Flowers, who held it over his head and prepared to throw it inbounds. Oscar Robertson, crouching, concealed himself behind a Muncie player and watched Flowers's eyes closely, searching for a clue as to where the pass was headed. When Flowers released the ball, Oscar sprang forward, stepped in front of Muncie's Jim Hinds, leaped high to pluck the ball out of the air, and then dribbled it around the court in circles until the time expired. When the buzzer sounded, Oscar flung the ball high into the fieldhouse rafters and leaped aboard his jubilant teammates.

Oscar Robertson cuts down the net after Attucks's victory in the 1955 regional round.
(*Indianapolis Recorder* Collection, Indiana Historical Society)

The victory put Attucks in the tournament's final four and threw Indianapolis's city officials into a dither. Who the next state champion would be now seemed a foregone conclusion. None of the other three teams remaining in the tourney—Theodore Roosevelt (an all-black school in Gary, popularly known as Gary Roosevelt), New Albany, or Fort Wayne North Side—seemed to stand a chance against the great Crispus Attucks Tigers. All signs said that Indianapolis would soon have its first state champion, and that champ would be an all-black school.

Indianapolis had one week to get ready. City officials, all white, prepared to prevent a race riot that would tear the town apart. Attucks's principal, Russell Lane, was among the first to understand that the city was getting ready not to crown the Tigers, but to sequester them once again. "The week before the finals, I got called into the superintendent's office," he later recalled. "There were representatives from the mayor's office and from the police and fire departments. The mayor's man said, 'Well, looks like your boys are going to win next week.' I said, 'We think so.' He said, 'We're afraid if they do, your people will break up the city.' I said, 'There will not be one incident.'"

Deeply offended but pragmatic, Dr. Lane spent much of the next

13 Negroes, 7 Whites Are Big Four Starters

When the Final Foursome of high school basketball teams take the floor at Butler Fieldhouse on Saturday, their starting lineups will include 13 Negro boys and 7 whites.

The squads as a whole will be made up of 23 colored lads and 17 of Caucasian ancestry.

The sepia player has come into his own as never before. This is the outstanding feature as the tournament heads for a very probable all-Negro finale.

Favored to meet in the championship game are Attucks of Indianapolis and Roosevelt of Gary —and there isn't a paleface among 'em.

Ever since the start of the season this newspaper has been writing about the possibility of several Negro teams making it to the last go-round. For our pains we have been accused of "race-baiting" and "trying to start a riot."

Nothing of the kind. To encourage Negro teams and players does

In the days before the final four teams were to compete in the 1955 state finals, the *Indianapolis Recorder* pointed out that at schools throughout Indiana, African Americans were succeeding in basketball as never before. (*Indianapolis Recorder*)

week addressing the student body. Yet again he found himself preparing black students for contact with the white world. This time he was explaining the rules that governed joy. "I told them that if a white student turned over a car in jubilation, it would likely be regarded as good-natured foolishness. But if a black student did the same, it could be held against them all as evidence of the Negro's violent nature."

As the Saturday of the state finals approached, city officials pulled extra police from the day and late shifts and detailed them to Monument Circle, where there would be a brief ceremony honoring the tournament winner. Over a hundred civil defense police and all the city's court bailiffs were assigned to traffic detail. Detectives were staked to Butler Fieldhouse.

The problem was that Indianapolis, a city in which people with dark skin and people with light skin had been kept apart for so long, now had no collective experience of mingling on a large scale in public. It might have been easier to plan for a protest demonstration or a boycott; at least there were rules of engagement for those activities. But how did whites prepare to thank black people publicly, especially in front of stores and theaters in which blacks were not allowed free movement? What would happen if white girls and black boys danced together? What if blacks got cocky and whites resentful? What if people got drunk? No one knew, and Alex Clark, the youngest mayor in Indianapolis's history, was not about to take chances. Approving the emergency forces and diverting the celebration to the black neighborhood were, as he saw it, responsible actions. "We really didn't know what was going to happen," he said later. "Those police were a booster shot."

On Saturday morning, March 19, 1955, the day of the state finals, the Attucks team had breakfast at Ray Crowe's home and then headed for Butler Fieldhouse, where fifteen thousand fans watched them defeat New Albany 79—67 in the first semi-final game. Gary Roosevelt slipped by Fort Wayne North in the second contest. It would be an all-black state championship game.

Under heavy police guard, the Attucks players were taken to a dormitory at Butler University to catch a few hours' rest between games. Uniformed officers stood by the front building and hallway entrances. Attucks guard Bill Hampton remembered leaving his room to go to the restroom and finding himself accompanied by a police officer. "What are you doing?" asked Hampton, startled. "Orders," his companion replied.

The Tigers were certain of victory. They had played together for years with this game in mind. By now, Butler Fieldhouse felt like a home court to them. And since all the players on both teams would be black, for once the referees' racial attitudes wouldn't matter. "We thought the refs might even give us a break since we were from Indianapolis," recalled Willie Merriweather. "That afternoon we were sayin' those rings are *ours*. We'll just go out there and beat those guys up."

To display citywide unity, one cheerleader from each of the other Indianapolis public and Catholic schools—eleven in all—went to Butler Fieldhouse that evening to form a delegation of support for Attucks. Wearing their school letter sweaters, they joined with the seven Attucks cheerleaders to rouse the giant Butler Fieldhouse crowd, cheering from center court when play stopped. Many years later, some Attucks players would still appreciate this as a welcoming and thoughtful gesture. "Inspiring even beyond the tournament itself was the sight of these 18 young people in their happy conga line," editorialized the *Indianapolis Recorder*. "You could see that distinctions of race, creed and color were utterly forgotten. How many of our problems would be solved overnight if these clear-eyed youths had their way!"

Bob Wait, Cheerleader

Cheerleaders from schools throughout the city joined the Attucks cheering squad in supporting the Tigers in the state tourney. Broad Ripple High's Bob Wait is at far right in this photo from the 1955 Crispus Attucks yearbook. (Courtesy Crispus Attucks Museum)

"I don't know how I got picked to be the cheerleader representing Broad Ripple High in the citywide delegation, but I was told by a teacher to put on my letter sweater and report to Butler that afternoon. We had very little time to rehearse with the Attucks cheerleaders. We just went to work, practicing their yells. They were very nice to us.

"Our job was to run out and cheer from the middle of the floor during time-outs. I knew that history was being made that night. It was so special, just electrifying. I had never cheered before so many people as at Butler Fieldhouse . . . And Attucks had a great, unstoppable team. I had the best seat in the house. It was not just another game. There seemed to be a togetherness among us; we got the whole city going. How great that was! I still remember one of their cheers:

Old King Cole told Old King Tut
If you can't yell for Attucks keep your big mouth shut
Hey, Hey, Big Team

"When the game was over I was asked to get on a fire truck with the players and go around [Monument] Circle. There was supposed to be a bonfire,

> but shortly after the Circle lap, we cheerleaders were pulled off the truck and driven back to Butler Fieldhouse. I didn't understand and I didn't like it. I still don't."

Gary Roosevelt had an excellent team, featuring Dick Barnett, who would later star for the NBA's New York Knicks, and Wilson Eison, who would later be named the state's outstanding senior, but they were overmatched. That evening, before a statewide television audience, sixteen-year-old Oscar Robertson proved himself a man among boys. He scored 30 points on an assortment of shots, most of them variations off the side-step fadeaway jump shot he had been practicing at Lockefield since he was a young boy. And when he was double-teamed, he always seemed to find an open man, tossing soft lead passes to teammates Willie Merriweather and Sheddrick Mitchell for flying layups. Attucks guards Bill Hampton and Bill Scott stole the ball again and again to trigger even more fast-break baskets.

Attucks took a 24—15 lead in the first quarter and widened that lead throughout. Attucks won the game 97—64, scoring 32 points more than any Indiana champion had ever scored in a state final game. Jubilant fans started singing the "Crazy Song" early in the fourth quarter.

In a brief ceremony at the fieldhouse, each player was awarded a championship ring, and Oscar Robertson and Willie Merriweather, as co-captains, hoisted the state championship basketball trophy above them for all to see. They had become the first state champions from Indianapolis and the first all-black team in U.S. history to win a racially open championship tournament.

Hair still wet from showering, the ten whooping boys danced out of Butler Fieldhouse into the frosty night and pulled one another aboard a crimson fire engine that was waiting outside the fieldhouse. The mayor's limousine was idling in front of them, and eight motorcycles in front of that. Behind them were several busloads of Attucks fans and dozens of cars.

The motorcade roared east on Forty-Ninth Street and turned south onto Meridian Street, toward the heart of the city. The players, some with basketball nets draped around their necks, sped past the homes in which their mothers, a decade out of the South, worked as domestics. The mayor himself employed Bill Scott's grandmother as a maid and nanny to clean the house and take care of his children. Windows filled with white faces as the sirens blared, and some residents ran out onto their wide front lawns, waving at the players as the truck sped by.

The motorcade, three miles long, headed for Monument Circle, a large brick-paved public gathering area in the center of downtown Indianapolis, where fifteen thousand black and white celebrants waited to greet them. Police had sealed off the east, west, and south entrances to the circle. There was only one way in and one way out. The vehicles took a single, counterclockwise lap around the nearly three-hundred-foot-tall monument to the state's soldiers and sailors, pausing briefly for Mayor Clark to hand Coach Crowe a key to the city on the monument steps. Girls ran toward the truck, flinging their arms around the players and trying to kiss them. Abruptly, the siren blared and the truck took off again.

The truck swung sharply back north and away from the multitude— which even now was being dispersed—and sped quickly onto Indiana Avenue, the city's black Broadway. Hearing the sirens, jubilant blacks poured from the jazz clubs and restaurants and surged toward the truck. People began to dance in the street. Motor traffic came to a standstill in front of the clubs, but the horns kept blowing.

The procession crawled toward Northwestern Park, in Frog Island, where thirty thousand black Hoosiers were waiting, many of them dancing in a chain around an enormous bonfire. Sparks leaped high

Victory! Indianapolis's champions carry their coach on their shoulders in jubilation. Oscar Robertson is second from left. (Frank Fisse/*Indianapolis Star/USA TODAY* Network)

in the air as loudspeakers played LaVern Baker's "Tweedlee Dee" over and over again. Police prowled the park's perimeter, and detectives combed the crowd. The players danced the night away—except for the greatest of them all.

Oscar Robertson found himself unable to enjoy the party. Though tearful friends and neighbors engulfed him in hugs of gratitude, though others pounded his back and slapped his palm and thanked him profusely, something about the parade gnawed at him.

Indianapolis had reneged on its promise to thoroughly toast the champions. A few days before the victory, Mayor Clark had promised reporters, "They can have anything if they win." But, as it turned out, "anything" didn't include a citywide parade through the downtown area. They were champions, but they were still segregated, still unwelcome, still outcast. It felt like they were champions of their neighborhood, not the whole city.

City officials had been more interested in preventing the riot they imagined than in celebrating Attucks's accomplishment. After what the Tigers had just accomplished for the entire city, Oscar felt cheated. Yes, the fire truck had been shiny and the bonfire awaiting them at Northwestern Park had been impressive, but he had

Jubilant Attucks fans celebrate their champions with a huge bonfire at Northwestern Park, in the Frog Island neighborhood. Some, including Oscar Robertson, expected a citywide parade, and felt disappointed and angry that the celebration was confined to the neighborhood.
(*Indianapolis Recorder* Collection, Indiana Historical Society)

Indy's first state champs and the city's decision not to allow a parade both receive top billing.
(*Indianapolis Recorder*)

Scholarship Fund Launched Instead Of Civic Rites

Attucks' state champion Tigers will have a scholarship fund established in their name and likely will stow away many a drumstick in coming weeks, but there will be no Big Parade as fans had expected.

City officials and Chamber of Commerce leaders extended Indianapolis' gratitude to Ray Crowe's boys in ceremonies at the school Thursday.

"This was not alone an Attucks' victory, but a victory for every one of the 450,000 people here in Indianapolis," Mayor Alex M. Clark told a convocation of students.

The Mayor presented a resolution adopted by the City Council, congratulating the Tigers. The Council members, City Clerk Grace Tanner and Assistant City Attorney Rufus Kuykendall were present.

Mayor Clark also presented the school a plaque on behalf of the Downtown Merchants Association. Officers of the association attending were President Allan W. Kahn, Manager Murray H. Morris and Assistant Manager Bowman Downey.

SUPERINTENDENT of Schools Herman L. Shibler estimated that "some 75,000 people were involved in the victory celebration last Saturday night."

"I was more impressed with Crispus Attucks as a champion than any other team I have ever seen," declared L. V. Phillips, IHSAA commissioner. He also praised Indianapolis' behavior, saying it had taken winning the title "in stride."

W. Henry Roberts, president of the Indianapolis Chamber of Commerce, announced the scholarship plan. "We could have done many things," he said, "but we felt that we wanted to do something of lasting benefit.

"We have asked our mem-
Continued on Page 7

Continued from Page 1

bership on a voluntary basis to contribute money to a scholarship fund to be turned over to Principal Russell A. Lane and used as he sees fit."

The scholarships will go to deserving Attucks graduates who may or may not be basketball players. This is in line with the IHSAA's policy forbidding material rewards for successful athletes.

Gold basketballs were presented to the players and coaches by Robert E. Kirby, chairman of the Chamber's athletic committee.

William H. Book, executive vice-president of the Chamber, and Wayne Whiffing, athletic vice-chairman, were introduced.

WHETHER ALL THIS can adequately substitute for the anticipated Downtown Parade and/or City-Wide Banquet, is a question for the fan in the street to determine.

CHAMPION COACH, CHAMPION MAYOR: Ray Crowe, Attucks Tigers, coach happily receives the "key" to an admiring city from courageous Mayor Alex Clark when the triumphant Tigers reached Monument Circle last Saturday night after bringing Indianapolis its first State basketball championship. Mayor Clark lent invaluable tangible and moral support to the team throughout the state tourney. Who isn't glad he's glad we won!

THE BOYS RECEIVE THE BACON: Oscar Robertson and Willie Merriweather, the most ferocious Tigers of the entire Crispus Attucks band that won the state basketball championship last Saturday night, smile for the cameras but clutch hard to the coveted championship trophy it took Indianapolis 45 years to win. Otto Albright, president of the IHSAA Board of Control, is presenting the state's highest athletic award. (Recorder Photo by Jim Cummings)

expected a parade downtown, a chance for blacks and whites to celebrate together, a chance for everyone to thank the talented young citizens who had just delivered their city from a forty-year curse. A half century later, it still stung. "Did they think we'd riot because we were primitive animals, beasts who could do nothing but destroy . . . ?" Oscar wrote in his 2003 autobiography. "It is hard to forgive them for this. I try, but I can't. We weren't savages. We were a group of civilized, intelligent young people who [had] . . . just won the biggest game in the history of Indianapolis basketball."

At an early hour, Oscar slipped away from the bonfire and caught a ride to his father's house. Bailey Robertson Sr. was surprised to hear the key in the lock and see his son in the doorway. "I remember Oscar came home about ten thirty," he recalled. "He got a sandwich and lay down on the living room floor. He said, 'Dad, they really don't want us,' and went to bed."

Helen Bledsoe

Many white fans in Indianapolis were grateful to Attucks for at last winning a title for Indianapolis. They were eager to share in the celebration, wherever it was. Helen Bledsoe was eight years old and living on Indianapolis's west side when Attucks won the title. She recalls that night as follows:

My mom and dad and I watched the championship game on TV. My dad rooted for Attucks because they were the Indianapolis team in the finals. You could feel his excitement grow throughout the game. When Attucks won, he jumped up from the couch and told us to get our coats. "Let's go downtown and celebrate!" he said. It wasn't exactly downtown, but a neighborhood park where there were a lot of trees. Soon we were in a long line of traffic. As we approached the park, the line slowed to a crawl. Black people lined both sides of the street, cheering and dancing and waving their hands. Horns were blaring. We seemed to be the only white people around. My mom was uncomfortable. She wouldn't let us get out of the car. I wasn't afraid. I was excited.

There was a gigantic bonfire at the park and lots of black people partying. We

Attucks's championship inspired many white Hoosiers. The Bledsoe family, residing in nearby Speedway, grabbed their coats and drove to the bonfire to help celebrate the Tigers' victory. Helen Bledsoe (middle), then eight years old, has drawn inspiration from Attucks's win throughout her life. (Courtesy Helen Bledsoe)

watched people celebrate, and then the traffic cleared and we drove back home. That was the start of my awareness of racial matters. I worked for social justice throughout my career. I started a health clinic downtown. Oscar Robertson made an impact on my mind that has lasted all through my life. I followed him all the rest of his basketball days. Why? He was apparently a good guy. A good student. On that night I saw him as an underdog making it to the top.

However, most of Oscar's teammates were jubilant that night. "It didn't bother me that whites didn't want to help us celebrate," recalled Bill Scott. "I was happy to get back into the neighborhood and share this with my people. This was the first time two all-black teams, coached by black coaches, had played. I said to myself, 'This is ours, not theirs.' I think most of my teammates felt that way."

How did Ray Crowe feel? He answered the reporter's question with a single word: "Relief."

It was a night no one would forget. Attucks had turned the tables in a sweet, special way, through basketball of all things, a ticket that maybe only people in Indiana could fully understand. The news quickly raced around the country. A fifty thousand—watt radio station in Fort Wayne broadcast the game to listeners in six midwestern states. Dozens of black newspapers picked up the story of Attucks's victory on the wire of the Associated Negro Press, including the *Pittsburgh Courier* and the *Chicago Defender*, and spread the word throughout U.S. cities. In those early days of the civil rights movement, eleven teenagers from Indianapolis had made winning a ball game an act of pride and defiance.

March 19, 1955, also saw another historic victory for African Americans in sports. On that same night, in Kansas City, Missouri, the University of San Francisco, led by Bill Russell, became the first integrated college basketball team to win a national championship with a majority of black starters.

And even as Oscar Robertson anguished over the rejection he felt, he and his teammates were entering the hearts of black athletes everywhere. Overnight, thousands and thousands of blacks who had never been to Indiana learned about the Attucks High School victory. The Tigers soon found out that their triumph was the first time in U.S. history that an all-black team had won an open sports tournament.

Back at the bonfire, Marcus Stewart Jr., a black Shortridge High School student who later succeeded his father as editor of the *Indianapolis Recorder*, found himself, like Oscar, struggling with mixed feelings on that frosty March night. As Marcus snake-danced around the fire and cheered and pumped his fists into the chilly air, his thoughts kept returning to his parents. His mom and dad had struggled for years to get the family out of Frog Island so that Marcus and his siblings could go to Shortridge, not Attucks. But now, in the heat of the blaze, the teenager found himself envying the Attucks students and wishing his parents had stayed in the neighborhood. "I kept thinking, 'Attucks means black,'" Stewart recalled. "'Attucks

"Attucks was *ours*!" Coach Crowe joins Attucks cheerleaders and mascot in celebration.
(Courtesy Mary Ogelsby)

means *us*.' That was the happiest day in the lives of a whole generation of blacks in Indianapolis. It was like when Joe Louis would knock
someone out and the Avenue would be full of people. But this was
better. Joe Louis belonged to everyone. Attucks was *ours*!"

Attucks cheerleader Evelyn Watkins Clarke leaps high to support the Tigers. (*Indianapolis Recorder* Collection, Indiana Historical Society)

Perfection

We didn't think of ourselves as black.
We just thought of ourselves as very, very good.

—Attucks cheerleader Maxine Coleman

On **January 20, 1956, Attucks** took the floor in Indianapolis at Arsenal Tech's gym for a game against Michigan City, a traditional Chicago-area powerhouse. Ray Crowe fretted about the contest. Michigan City entered the game ranked by pollsters tenth in the state, with an 8—4 record achieved against tough, big-city competition. Crowe recalled that it was just about this time last year when Attucks had hit a slump, losing to Connersville. He worried the team would be flat.

He wasn't worried long. The Tigers hit their first seven shots and scored an astounding 39 points in the first eight minutes—a point every twelve seconds. They kept right on playing at a level that perhaps no high school team had ever achieved, winning 123—59. They realized they were playing on a high school squad that could beat many college teams.

Attucks forward Stanford Patton remembers seeing a white opponent crying after their game against Attucks. "The boy's daddy walked up to him and said, 'You might as well stop that crying. Because can't nobody beat them. You ought to be glad you ever played against them.'"

A few months after the 1955 state finals, Ray Crowe set out to replace seven graduating players from Attucks's state championship team. He was proud that four of them—Bill Scott, Bill Hampton, Sheddrick Mitchell, and Willie Merriweather—had landed full athletic scholarships to major colleges. From the swarm of boys who had tried out for the 1955—56 varsity team, Crowe chose Bill Brown and Stan Patton to provide rebounding and points up front. He also selected Albert Maxey, Edgar Searcy, Odell Donel, John Gipson, James Enoch, and guards Henry Robertson (Oscar's brother), LeVern Benson, and Sam Milton to fill out the lineup. The team did not have a lot of varsity experience, but it had a great deal of talent.

Attucks's lone returning senior was being hailed widely as the greatest player in Indiana's history and maybe the best high school player in America. Now seventeen, Oscar Robertson had grown yet another inch and packed on a few more pounds of muscle over the summer working on a construction crew. He now stood a powerful six-five. The team's overall height allowed Crowe to position Oscar at guard again, taking full advantage of his court vision and leadership. "Nobody, I mean nobody, saw the whole court like Oscar," marveled teammate Edgar Searcy. "He seemed not only to know where every offensive and defensive player was on the court but also where they were going, what they would do next. He knew who to get the ball to, and when to just keep it for himself."

The 1955—56 Attucks team set a goal to become the first Indiana high school team to go through an entire season—including the tournament—undefeated. To do so, they would have to win thirty-one consecutive games. They were out to set a new standard of excellence.

Now suiting up in eye-catching jade-and-gold jerseys featuring enlarged numbers above the word "Tigers," Attucks won their first eleven games before mammoth crowds. Attucks was usually far ahead by the time late-arriving fans were seated. Indianapolis Tech came closest, losing by a mere 7 points.

One episode just before the tournament started showed how dominant a player Oscar Robertson had become. Oscar had snapped Hallie Bryant's Indianapolis city record for most points in a single game when he scored 45 against Michigan City. But a week later Jerry Lawlis, a senior at George Washington High, poured in 48 points in an 87—85 overtime win against Speedway. Overnight, the blond-haired, blue-eyed sharpshooting Lawlis became the toast of the city, hailed as "the greatest scorer in Indianapolis history." His shooting hand, likened to a rifle, was celebrated by the *Indianapolis Times* as "the most wicked left hand you ever saw."

Fans wondered: Would Oscar take Lawlis's feat as a challenge? Would he respond? Would Ray Crowe let Oscar try to recapture his record? Did Oscar care about it? Did he even *know* about it? Just before Attucks's next-to-last pre-tournament game, against Sacred Heart High, Crowe gathered his team in the locker room and put the question to them: Should we give Oscar the chance to get his record back?

Oscar was given no input into the decision.

The answer was obvious from the game's opening whistle. Whenever Oscar would pass the ball, the receiving teammate would snap it right back to him. No one would take a shot. With no choice, Oscar went to work. He scored 20 of Attucks's 23 points in the first quarter. He shot and scored from all over the court. As the *Indianapolis Recorder* put it, "He hit from under, from slightly out, from out and from way out. He hit the layups, the hooks, the shovels, the jumps and the set shots. He was superb." And when he was finished, Oscar Robertson had scored 62 points in a thirty-two-minute game. And he was, of course, once again the sole owner of the city of Indianapolis's scoring record.

Oscar Robertson and Ray Crowe examine the Indianapolis News *Basketball Record Book*, much of which they had just rewritten. (Indiana Basketball Hall of Fame)

• • •

During the early days of 1956, Indianapolis newspapers were filled with stories about the ongoing Montgomery, Alabama, bus boycott. Clearly, some southern black citizens were no longer willing to accept the inferior places and roles assigned to them. On December 1, 1955, forty-two-year-old seamstress Rosa Parks of Montgomery had been arrested when she refused to surrender her seat at the front of the "colored section" of a bus to a white passenger. In response, Montgomery's black community organized an alternative transportation system and stopped riding the city buses. On December 21, 1956, a federal court order desegregated Montgomery's buses. The order came after a hearing in which four women, led by a courageous sixteen-year-old high school junior named Claudette Colvin, convincingly testified as to the abuses they had experienced while riding the buses.

In Indianapolis, the Montgomery bus boycott shared headline space and column inches with a high school basketball team. As Purdue University historian Randy Roberts put it, "The main stories in Montgomery and Indianapolis were part of the same long, progressive struggle for justice and advancement. There may have been some corner of Indiana where basketball was just basketball, but that corner was not the west side of Indianapolis. There basketball was sacred, connecting to notions of racial progress, racial pride and racial accomplishments."

It was hard for many white Hoosiers who grew up hearing and assuming that whites were better than blacks to accept that Attucks was undefeated and maybe undefeatable. How could inferior people be unbeatable? One widely held idea among whites was expressed something like this: "Well, okay, some blacks might be *physically* superior, but they are not as intelligent as whites."

But Oscar Robertson—the African American figure white Hoosiers

Indianapolis Recorder

INDIANA'S GREATEST WEEKLY

Entered at the Post Office, Indianapolis, Indiana as Second-Class Matter Under the Act of March 7, 1870   POSTAL ZONE 7

61st. Year   Phone ME. 4-1545   Indianapolis, Indiana, Feb. 18, 1956   Number 7

PRICE 10 CENTS

Health Thief Deals Postman Underhand Blow

MARVIN E. POWELL

ATTUCKS vs. 741 OTHERS

Attucks Favored To Capture 2nd Straight Title

By JIM CUMMINGS

Crispus Attucks' state champs, riding a string of 34 consecutive wins and shooting for their second straight Hoosier hoop crown, draw Beech Grove as their first-round opponent in an Indianapolis Sectional which Tiger opponents say is "built to order" for Attucks.

The Tigers, ranked No. 1 throughout the season in all the statewide polls, were expected to have very little trouble with Beech Grove, which comes to the tournament with a record of five wins in 17 games.

Attucks meets the small county school at 8:15 Thursday night.

In the so-called "weak" bottom bracket with the Tigers are Indianapolis Wood School, Howe, Deaf School, Cathedral, Manual and Washington.

Washington and Manual regarded as Attucks' biggest threats in his bracket, crash head-on Friday morning in the last game of the first round. The winner could meet Attucks in the semi-final game Saturday morning. Attucks will have to get by Beech Grove and the winner of the Deaf School-Cathedral game to get to the semis.

TECH AND SHORTRIDGE, in the teams practically everyone agrees have the best chance of upsetting the Tigers, will fight one another in the very first game of the local tourney. The teams, each of whom gave Attucks two close battles during the season, meet the curtain at 6 p.m. Wednesday.

Friends of Tech and Shortridge feel their teams, by having to meet in the first game, are sacrificing an unfair fate. They say Attucks, by virtue of the already weak caliber of the teams in the Tiger bracket, has a free ticket to the community.

EXTRA!

Featured in this edition is a full page of pictures of teams competing in the Indianapolis Sectional with the Attucks Tigers. SEE PAGE 9, also page 11 for additional pictures and stories.

DEFENDING STATE CHAMPS: Crispus Attucks' defending state basketball champions who are favorites to capture their fifth sectional title in six years are shown above. They are first row (left to right), William Brown, Herbert Swangon, Lavenne Benson, Sam Milton, Albert Maxey and Henry Robertson. Standing are Coach Roy Crowe, Odell Donel, Edgar Searcy, John Gipson, Oscar Robertson, Stanford Patton and James Enoch.

Victors Over Tavern Form Organization

Anti-Negro Riot at U. of Alabama Spotlights Desegregation Battle

ATLANTA, Ga.—The Autherine Lucy riots at the University of Alabama have centered national attention on the final outcome of the desegregation movement — how soon?

Demos Ask Ike To Head Off School Aid Tilt

WASHINGTON, D. C.—A group of right House Democrats sought a way to prevent a bitter fight on an amendment to the school construction bill.

Many GOP's To Honor Lincoln, Douglass

TV Show to Raise Funds To Fight Dread Disease

Univ. of Alabama To Fight Opening School to Negroes

BIRMINGHAM, Ala.—The University of Alabama which has accepted a federal court order admitting Miss Autherine Lucy several days ago, now has decided to appeal that decision pending her release suspension last week.

Racial Tension High As Bus Boycott Continues

MONTGOMERY, Ala.—While the cost of the 16-weeks-old bus boycott by Negroes is a matter not being made public by the National City Bus Lines, or the cost to the community by civic leaders calculated, racial tension between Negroes and whites runs high.

GA. NEWSPAPERMAN TO SPEAK AT RALLY HERE

William Gordon, managing editor of the Atlanta (Ga.) Daily World, will be guest speaker at a public mass meeting at Mt. Paran Baptist Church, 12th and Missouri streets, Sunday, Feb. 19, at 3 p.m.

Free Tax Service

The defending champs were the heavy favorites going into the 1956 tourney. (*Indianapolis Recorder*)

Attucks Favored To Capture 2nd Straight Title

By JIM CUMMINGS

Crispus Attucks' state champs, riding a string of 34 consecutive wins and shooting for their second straight Hoosier hoop crown, drew Beech Grove as their first-round opponent in an Indianapolis Sectional which Tiger opponents say is "built to order" for Attucks.

The Tigers, ranked No. 1 throughout the season in all the statewide polls, were expected to have very little trouble with Beech Grove, which comes to the tournament with a record of five wins in 17 games.

Attucks meets the small county school at 8:15 Thursday night.

In the so-called "weak" bottom bracket with the Tigers are Harry E. Wood School, Howe, Deaf School, Cathedral, Manual and Washington.

Washington and Manual, regarded as Attucks' biggest threats in its bracket, crash head-on Friday morning in the last game of the first round. The winner could meet Attucks in the semi-final round Saturday morning. Attucks will have to get by Beech Grove and the winner of the Deaf School-Cathedral game to get to the semis.

TECH AND SHORTRIDGE, the two teams practically everyone agrees have the best chance of upsetting the Tigers, will fight one-another in the very first game of the local tourney. The teams, each of whom gave Attucks two close battles during the season, raise the curtain at 6 p.m. Wednesday.

Friends of Tech and Shortridge feel their teams, by having to meet in the first game, are suffering unfair fates. They say Attucks, by virtue of the allegedly weak caliber of the teams in the Tiger bracket, has a free ticket

Continued on Page 7

to the final game of the Sectional.

Emotions are always high in Indiana this time of year as Hoosier Hysteria reaches a Mt. Everest high . . . But memories seem to get shorter as the years wear on.

Records show that nothing is certain.

Nobody is "booked to win."

When the boys start throwing that fall up there in pursuit of the world's biggest basketball bauble, every school's five boys is automatically transformed into a team.

There are 742 in the field this time out and not one rolls over dead under the weight of opponents' press clippings. Brother, they all have to be "showed."

A quickie glimpse at Recorder records shows that in 1953, the mighty Greenclads of Tech were "booked to win" the local sectional. Tech had beaten Muncie Central and Richmond while running up an 18-2 season record and when tourney firing got underway the Techites were rated No. 2 in the whole state and had finished second in the rough North Central Conference.

They got slaughtered in the first game of the sectional by "little" Ben Davis.

Then Attucks, after winning the sectional that year, was favored to go on to the state crown. But it happened in the regional. Shelbyville was awarded a decision as officials tooted a last-seconr call against Hallie Bryant.

Anything can happen in Indiana basketball, and everything usually does around tournament time.

If Attucks wins the sectional . . . (pause here briefly).

This writer looked over the Tiger roster last year, right after Attucks brought Indianapolis its first state championship, then checked the '56 potential of the other state powerhouses and finally predicted (in print) way back then that the Tigers would repeat as state champions this time. And he has not changed his mind.

Anyway, if the Tigers swoop successfully through the sectional, as we have no doubts they will, they will become the winning'est teams in the history of Indiana basketball (provided, of course, they made it past Frankfort Friday night).

The necessary four wins in the first week of the tournament would give Attucks a 39-straight winning record. The current record is 38 straight, set by Vincennes (1922-23) and equalled by Frankfort (1935-37).

Should the Tigers go all the way this time, their record will stand at an amazing 45 wins without a loss.

The Tigers, prior to the Frankfort game, had amassed what is probably one of the most sensational six-season records of all time in Hoosier prep circles.

RAY CROWE took over the coaching reins at the school at the start of the 1950-51 season and since then the teams have won 141 games and lost only 14. They have won four sectionals (three straight), annexed three regionals, two semi-finals and topped this all off with the state crown last year.

Not bad, eh, for a team which was accepted into the Indiana High School Athletic Association only 12 years ago? All the other schools, except the Negro and the Catholic schools, have been members of the IHSAA throughout the organization's 44-year history.

knew best—was especially troublesome to this notion because he brilliantly and obviously conducted traffic on the court. It was his game. Those who didn't know him had no idea that his mastery of basketball derived as much from a matchless understanding of the game as to physical attributes such as height, leaping ability, and foot speed. Oscar Robertson had been studying the team game— the game inside the game—since he was a young boy. He was like a chess prodigy who saw possibilities and traps several steps in advance. He had been mentored by some of the smartest players and coaches in Indianapolis. They had recognized his promise early on and had shown him all they knew. Beyond that, the polite and serious young man was neatly dressed, clean shaven, and well spoken. Newspapers reported that Oscar was a B+ student, taking Algebra 4. His class grade rank was within the top ten percent at Attucks. He aspired to be an engineer.

It was just plain hard to view someone like that as inferior.

Early in March, Attucks entered the 1956 Indiana High School Boys Basketball Tournament with a record of twenty-one wins and no losses. The Tigers were so dominant that they had never been behind in the second half of a game. Ray Crowe felt intense, jaw-popping pressure not to lose, not to be eliminated from the tourney, not to let the community down. Hopes and expectations had ballooned.

Attucks began the tournament by rolling over Beech Grove High 91—30 and then defeating Indianapolis Howe 72—58. Eight wins to go. Next up was Indianapolis Cathedral, a Catholic school with a special connection to Attucks, for both had been banned from the tourney years before. During their exile, the two schools had played each other nearly every year. But there was no sentiment during the Saturday afternoon semi-final at Butler when the referee blew his whistle and tossed the ball in the air. A scrappy Cathedral team kept the contest close throughout. Oscar, playing much of the second half with four fouls, drove to the basket, pulled up, and hit several clutch shots down the stretch to seal an Attucks victory.

A few hours later, Attucks hung on to defeat Indianapolis Short-ridge in a grueling thriller, 53—48. The win was Attucks's thirty-ninth consecutive victory amassed over the span of two seasons, breaking an Indiana record that had stood since 1922. There were brief poses for photographers' flashbulbs but no time for celebrating. Time now was for sleep. Six wins to go.

The next weekend, Attucks beat Anderson 61—48 in the Indianapolis regional round's opening game. In the second game, with Attucks well ahead of Hancock Central, Oscar drove hard for the basket, leaped high above the others, and laid the ball in the hoop. He came down on a player who had slid underneath him. Oscar spun head over heels and put his right hand out to brace the fall. He landed with the full weight of his body on his right wrist, his shooting hand. The giant Butler Fieldhouse crowd fell silent as Oscar rose slowly from the floor and walked off court, wearing a pained expression and supporting his right wrist with his left hand.

"I thought maybe it was broken," Ray Crowe recalled.

An enlarged photograph of Oscar Robertson's bandaged wrist pushed aside world and national news photos in the *Recorder*. But X-rays proved negative, and Robertson was back in the lineup for the semi-final games against Connersville and Scottsburg, both of which Attucks won handily.

Now the Tigers were in the final four once again, surviving a field that had started with 743 teams a full month before. Two wins to go. They were heavy favorites. Indianapolis officials huddled once again to consider how the city might celebrate another Attucks victory. Last year, they had given Attucks the moon and stars—at least that's how they saw it. They had hosted several banquets. The Chamber of Commerce had established a scholarship fund in Attucks's name. The Downtown Merchants' Association had given the team a plaque. The mayor, who had watched the final game in the Attucks cheering section, had passed a resolution thanking Attucks for winning the title with "outstanding ability, fine sportsmanship, and gentlemanly conduct." And, of course, there had been the fire-truck lap around Monument Circle and the jubilant motorcade to a colossal bonfire in Northwestern Park. What more could they want?

Superintendent of Schools Herman Shibler proudly estimated that, all in all, 75,000 people had celebrated with the Tigers the year before. But the *Recorder* pointed out that that was a mere fraction of the city's 450,000 residents. Indiana's first undefeated champions deserved the Big Parade—as they called it—in broad daylight through the city's wide downtown streets, to give all the team's fans a chance to see the heroes up close and offer them the thanks they deserved. Northwestern Park again? Most whites had never even heard of Northwestern Park, and, had they known where it was, many would never have visited it at night. If whites were to share in the pride of a victory that benefited everyone, the event should be celebrated downtown in daylight. A poll of *Recorder* readers reported that most favored a daytime citywide parade over a late-night neighborhood bonfire.

But officials fell back on the same timorous format as the year before: a motorcade from Butler Fieldhouse downtown, a brisk lap around the Monument Circle, a bonfire at Northwestern Park, and home to bed. It worked last year, they told one another, and might well have prevented trouble. If Attucks can win again, the same celebration should be plenty good enough for them. Amen.

In the first of the tournament's two afternoon final four games, Lafayette Jefferson High, ranked second behind Attucks most of the

Oscar Robertson shows his sprained thumb, an injury he incurred against Anderson High in the 1956 regional tournament.
(*Indianapolis Star*/William Palmer/*Indianapolis News*, Indiana Historical Society/*USA TODAY* Network)

year, squeezed by Elkhart High 52—50 at Butler Fieldhouse in Indianapolis. Attucks took the court against Terre Haute Gerstmeyer for the second afternoon game and held on to win 68—59 even though Oscar fouled out with eleven minutes remaining in the game. Exhausted, the Tigers made their way back to dormitory rooms on Butler's campus for a brief rest.

One game to go.

A few hours later, Attucks returned to Butler Fieldhouse to face Lafayette Jefferson High for a chance at their second straight state title, and Indiana's first perfect season. The fieldhouse gates opened, and fans surged through, most of them hiking up to the fieldhouse rafters, pausing every few steps to look back and catch their breath.

The Crispus Attucks Tigers emerged from the locker room and jogged out onto the gleaming court, resplendent in their full dress-white warm-up suits.

On the other end of the fieldhouse floor, ten white, crew-cut boys representing Jefferson High School, from the northern Indiana city of Lafayette, were also jogging through their warm-up drills. Jeff was a traditional powerhouse in Indiana, coached by Marion Crawley,

In the championship game of the 1956 tourney, Attucks and Jefferson players scramble for a loose ball (left), and Oscar Robertson goes up for the final 2 points of the game, which Attucks won 79–57 (above). (*Indianapolis Star*/William Palmer/*Indianapolis News*, Indiana Historical Society/*USA TODAY* Network)

who, having won three state titles, was revered as one of the most successful coaches in the state's history. Lafayette Jefferson had been ranked second in the polls to Attucks for most of the year.

When the horn sounded, the starting Attucks five—Robertson, Patton, Brown, Maxey, and Searcy—peeled off their warm-up gear and walked out onto the court to shake hands with their opponents and take positions around the midcourt circle. Oscar won the tipoff, took a return pass on the right side of the basket, ball-faked his defender out of position, and sank a soft one-handed jump shot. All of nine seconds were gone.

Lafayette took the ball out of bounds, and one of their guards

Oscar Robertson ringed by cheerleaders after the 1956 championship. (*Indianapolis Star*/William Palmer/*Indianapolis News*, Indiana Historical Society/*USA TODAY* Network)

walked the ball up the court. Jefferson probed the perimeter of Attucks's tight, shifting zone defense with a series of two-handed chest passes, whipping the ball inside now and then but passing it back out as Attucks collapsed on the ball. It was an attack with cobwebs. Attucks rebounded a missed shot and scored quickly again, causing Lafayette Jefferson to become even more mothballed, passing the ball thirty-four times before daring their next shot.

The game was over before it started, with Attucks rebounding missed shots and sprinting the ball down the floor in waves for easy baskets. Once again, Attucks presented the future of basketball—fast, creative, airborne, one-handed, and opportunistic. Attucks won 79—57, becoming the first undefeated state champion since the tournament began in 1911.

Fans started singing the "Crazy Song" at the end of the third quarter.

Oscar Robertson shattered Indiana's previous individual scoring mark in a state championship game by scoring 39 points and making it look easy. In a few brief months, he would be known throughout the nation as "the Big O," the best college basketball player in the land. His final high school game was a valentine to the fans, a performance that in the future would remind them there had once been a player in Indiana of such consummate excellence.

After the game, Lafayette coach Marion Crawley was asked about Attucks's star player. Crawley shook his head. "That Oscar Robertson is the greatest high school player I have seen in all my years of coaching," he told reporters. "He'll kill you anywhere because he can do anything. There just isn't any way to stop him."

After showering, the Attucks players again skipped out of Butler Fieldhouse, clasped hands, and pulled one another aboard the fire

The fire-truck parade after the 1956 state title. It was the same story as the year before: a hasty loop around a downtown monument and then a sprint to the Attucks neighborhood. Oscar is at left, with his hands in the air, standing next to Bill Brown, also in a letterman jacket. (*Indianapolis Star*/William Palmer/*Indianapolis News*, Indiana Historical Society/*USA TODAY* Network)

The *Recorder* hails the two-time champs with highlights from the citywide celebration.
(*Indianapolis Recorder*)

truck idling in the lot. They zipped up their green-and-gold letter jackets against the sting of the night and found secure places as the motorcade started off. The vehicles shot down Meridian Street, then slowed as they reached the great spire of the Indiana Soldiers and Sailors Monument, built to honor those Hoosiers who had fought in the Revolutionary War, the Civil War, and the Spanish-American War. There, Oscar did something impulsive. He leaped off the truck and ran up the dozens of steps to the monument's south face. Reaching the top, he turned and waved at the crowd for a moment; then he ran down and leaped back aboard as the motorcade pushed off for Northwestern Park and a bonfire. Along the way, the champions waved and smiled and brandished their championship rings for the cheering, reaching, fist-pumping crowd to see.

Minutes later, the Crispus Attucks Tigers pulled into the park, the vehicles carefully parting the sea of fans. On that cold night, the crowd was warmed by the knowledge that Attucks had not only won but had done so in the grandest of style. They had won each of their thirty games—actually, forty-five wins in a row when you counted last year's season-ending victory string. They were the first undefeated champions in the forty-six-year history of the tournament. They were so dominant that no team all year long had led Attucks in the second half of a game. They had claimed the title *and* raised the bar, perhaps beyond reach. No one could ever take that away.

Theirs was a performance that could be equaled but never surpassed.

They were a team for the ages.

The 1955 state champs, from the Attucks High School yearbook. (Crispus Attucks Museum, IUPUI University Library digital collections)

Legacy

10

Oscar was like our Rosa Parks.

—Ray Tolbert, a black player who grew up in Indiana in the 1960s

So, **thinking back to Oscar's contention**, the one that inspired this book: Did the great Crispus Attucks High School basketball teams accelerate the racial integration of Indianapolis? Integration certainly started slowly enough. The state's desegregation law of 1949 allowed—but didn't force—black students to attend their neighborhood schools. Black students could still opt to go to Attucks, no matter where they lived in Indianapolis. For a while, almost all black students kept to family tradition and went to Attucks. But once

Attucks started winning, other coaches of city schools began to recruit black players. "Break up the Attucks dynasty!" Ray Crowe recalled everyone saying. And for the first time, he found himself competing against other city schools for athletes. The competition tightened year by year.

"The success of Attucks's basketball integrated the high schools of Indianapolis," said sportswriter Bob Collins flatly. "They became so dominant that the other schools had to get black basketball players or forget about it . . . [They] went from not caring to crying, 'Unfair!' They were even saying, 'This is *illegal!*' They were saying, 'Oscar lives in the Shortridge district and Hallie Bryant should be going to Tech.' In 1951, I don't think any other team in Marion County had a black player." By 1955, Shortridge had four black starters. By 1956, as black families continued to expand into Indianapolis neighborhoods, Tech High had 769 black students and Shortridge had 657 black students. As Collins put it, "Integration was just making a slow start, and Attucks's basketball success speeded it."

Some also contend that Attucks's success opened doors to the city's restaurants and softened resistance to the presence of blacks in downtown stores and theaters. "We gave the black community hope," said Oscar Robertson. "[We] heard talk about how blacks were lazy, how they don't want to get up and go to work, how they have too many kids. But when Attucks started to win, they could brag on us. There were people in the city who got up in the morning and felt good about themselves when they looked in the mirror. All because of what Crispus Attucks had done."

And many believe that Attucks's success changed the way blacks and whites came to view one another. Attucks forward Stanford Patton said, "I don't think it had ever happened before, that the whole city got behind one team. That showed me something. I knew they didn't really have to like us, but they had to respect us for what we did and how we did it . . . We destroyed a lot of myths—that a black man couldn't out-coach a white man, that we would break under pressure, that we was cowards. That was the perception people were introduced to, that even we blacks had believed."

Some hearts and minds were being tested in the privacy of people's living rooms. One twelve-year-old sixth-grade girl watched the televised 1955–56 tournament games with her family on Indianapolis's west side. Her family, like many other white families, struggled with what they were seeing on the television screen. "The N-word was used, quite a bit, by my dad. When Attucks would score, my dad would curse. And he was a well-educated person, more open-minded than most around where we lived. That championship game definitely made us gain respect for blacks. My parents had to admit that they were worth something. Oscar in particular seemed a role model, maybe just because he was the best player, but also just the way he was."

For black boys and girls, Oscar Robertson was a superhero. "He was like our Rosa Parks," said Ray Tolbert, later a star player at Indiana University. George McGinnis, a black Indianapolis high school star who became an NBA Hall of Famer, watched the 1955 Attucks— Gary Roosevelt championship on TV with his entire family yelling and screaming support at the set. "[Oscar] was our prince, our standard-bearer," McGinnis recalled. "He was the guy every African American kid who picked up a basketball from that point on emulated."

But despite the joy and goodwill, hard times set in for blacks in Indianapolis during the years after the Attucks wins. In the 1960s, city authorities bulldozed many of the houses in Frog Island to make room for an expansion of a hospital and a college campus. City officials called the operation "urban renewal." Blacks called it "Negro removal." Longtime residents were given but a few months to clear out and find other places to live. Some were paid a pittance, others nothing at all. "It's the only time I ever saw my dad cry, when he got that notice," said Pat Payne, a 1957 graduate of Shortridge High.

About half of the apartment buildings in Lockefield Gardens were demolished. Others were converted to condominiums and sold primarily to whites at steep prices. The Dust Bowl court at Lockefield was demolished without even a marker to show where it had been or to record what it had meant to the development of basketball. Though the black population of Indianapolis continued to grow, prospects for black political power were weakened by a state law passed in 1969 that, in effect, encouraged whites to move to suburbs and abandon the inner city. Black voting power was cut almost in half. Crime and drug abuse increased.

Community leaders fought fiercely to save Crispus Attucks High. The first white students enrolled in 1971, but by then it was a far different school than it was in 1954, when the Supreme Court ordered the desegregation of the nation's public schools. As African American students were bused to the suburbs, Attucks's best teachers were also removed from Attucks and scattered in schools throughout the city. A major highway slashed through the neighborhood, further isolating families. Attucks's enrollment plummeted, and closure was considered. Some proposed demolishing the building. The community rallied and kept the school standing. Attucks was converted from a high school to a junior high school in 1986. The varsity basketball program was shut down.

The closing of Attucks as a high school was an agonizing blow to the community. "Many of my fondest memories are associated with that school," said Ray Crowe. "But if you look at it another way, maybe the closing of Crispus Attucks marked the end of a sick social experiment . . . Maybe something good can come of it."

Somehow during the next decade the school remained standing, even through periods of disuse. It reverted back to a middle school in 1993 and remained so until 2006, when Indianapolis school superintendent Eugene White announced the formation of the Crispus Attucks Medical Magnet High School. It now attracts students throughout the city who wish to become veterinarians, crime-scene forensic specialists, practitioners of sports medicine, or other types of medical professionals. The move took advantage of Attucks's closeness to the campus of Indiana University School of Medicine and associated hospitals. Attucks is still a largely black school, with its student body around sixty percent African American, thirty percent Latino, and ten percent white. It offers both college prep and vocational classes.

The Attucks basketball program was restored in 2008. By then, the Indiana high school tournament had undergone a huge change. In 1998, Indiana's sports authorities divided the tournament into four classes based on school enrollment. The change put the state in turmoil. Legends such as Oscar Robertson announced their opposition to the change. After eighty-seven years, the Hoosier State's small schools would never again have the opportunity to topple a big-city Goliath, as tiny Milan High had done in 1954. The change was especially hard to swallow for fans who had lived in Indiana a long time. But there it was, love it or leave it: in the new world, Attucks belonged not to the entire state, but to Class 3-A, among the next-to-biggest schools.

Josiah Herndon, Attucks Class of 2017

Josiah Herndon was a recent student at the Crispus Attucks Medical Magnet School. He says:

> I could have gone to any high school. I chose Attucks because it gives you a

chance to start college early. You can earn high school credits in middle school. By high school you can be earning college credits.

My goal is to be a forensic scientist, working with crime-scene evidence on murder cases, looking at evidence like bullet casings and blood spatters. Attucks is a perfect fit for me. I've taken lots of science courses like biology, chemistry, and physics. The lab equipment is first rate. Next year I will attend Purdue University.

Even in grade six I knew Attucks was a historically black school. Then in middle school we took a tour of the Attucks museum in social studies class. That really broke it down.

My family is from Mississippi and Chicago, so I don't have relatives in the classroom photos in Attucks's hallways. But those photos have sparked an interest in me. All those people really walked the same hallways that I do now, way back in the 1920s. It shows our connection. Attucks is resilient. They put all those obstacles in our path, to try to make us fail, and each time we prevail.

I love basketball. I'm the student manager on the Attucks basketball team. We're ranked number five in the state, with a 13–4 record. It means a lot that someone from Attucks— Oscar Robertson—made it very big in the world. Yes, he's an NBA legend,

Josiah Herndon, Crispus Attucks Medical Magnet High School class of 2017. (Courtesy Josiah Herndon)

but he started here, at Attucks. I've never had a chance to meet him, but it still motivates me.

What would I say to someone considering enrollment at Attucks? It's a great place to be, but get ready to work. Classes are not a joke. They're really trying to get you going here.

Jamal Harris of Crispus Attucks puts up the game-winning shot over Blake Bennington of Twin Lakes in the 2017 Class 3-A State Finals at Bankers Life Fieldhouse in Indianapolis. (John Terhune/ *Journal & Courier* via AP)

So Attucks went to work. In March 2014, the school claimed its first Indianapolis sectional title since 1973. Winning was an old habit, and it still felt great. The Tigers were eliminated the following week in their regional tournament, but the sectional success had given them something to build on.

It took only three years for the dividend to arrive. On Saturday, March 25, 2017, Attucks's high-flying junior Jamal Harris leaped for a rebound and guided a shot back into the basket less than a second before the game-ending buzzer sounded, giving the Tigers a 73—71 win over Twin Lakes for the state Class 3-A title. Among the thousands of jubilant celebrants who leaped to their feet in Bankers Life Field-house was Oscar Robertson, white-haired, thickset, and now seventy-eight years of age. He doesn't jump much these days, but it was Attucks's first state boys' championship since 1959. Oscar, the

Seventy-eight-year-old Oscar Robertson bestows the 2017 state championship medal on Jamal Harris, the six-two guard who scored the winning basket for Attucks. (*Indianapolis Star/USA TODAY* Network)

basketball legend now universally known as "the Big O," turned to the crowd and raised his hands high after Harris's buzzer-beating shot. Afterward, he proudly placed the championship medals around the necks of the winners. "This is almost like a movie script," Robertson remarked.

The headline in the next day's *Indianapolis Star* shouted, "Crispus Attucks' state title is 'bigger than basketball.'"

In the end, the precise legacy of the great Indianapolis Crispus Attucks teams of the 1950s is hard to measure. It is found most clearly in the spirit and memory of those who passed through those times together. The hallways of Crispus Attucks High are still lined with the class photos of generations of black Indianapolis students, composites of parents and aunts and uncles and cousins. "That's my great-aunt," an escort told me on a tour of the school. "And there's my maternal grandmother."

If walls could talk, Attucks's would be worth listening to. They'd know the "Crazy Song" for sure. They could tell the almost scriptural tales of Flap's shot, Oscar's steal against Muncie, the death threats

The Parade That Wasn't

Oscar Robertson has said he might never forgive Indianapolis for routing the state championship celebratory parade away from downtown in 1955 and 1956. City officials have tried several times to make up for the slight. In 2015, the surviving players from the 1955 Attucks championship team climbed aboard a float and, with their cheerleaders at their sides, took part in a daylight parade that included a trip around Monument Circle. Oscar Robertson attended, but he withheld comment. And in April 2017, players and coaches from the Attucks Class 3-A championship team were honored, along with boys and girls champions from the other divisions, by a parade around Monument Circle and a guest appearance at an Indiana Pacers NBA basketball game.

The year 2017 marked the first time in the class basketball era, dating back to 1998, that three Indianapolis teams reached the state finals in the same season.

In 2015, the surviving players from Attucks's 1955 championship team, and their cheerleaders, were celebrated in a parade through downtown Indianapolis. Oscar Robertson stands in the foreground. (*Indianapolis Star/USA TODAY* Network)

before the Tech game, and referee Dubis's outrageous call against Hallie. They would tell the remarkable story of a close-knit community, led by hardworking Indiana teenagers who, in the course of a decade, awakened their city, jolting many residents into an acceptance of racial diversity they weren't prepared to make. The Attucks story is above all a ringing example of the powerful and undervalued contributions young people have made to U.S. history.

If walls could talk, the Attucks halls would surely, at various times, shout and sob and ring with laughter. For it may be that, more than any other building in the state, Crispus Attucks High School, still standing proudly at 1140 Dr. Martin Luther King Jr. Street, once again home of champions and still educating the youth of Indianapolis after nearly a century, has known Hoosiers at their most hysterical—and their most magnificent.

Acknowledgments

First, I thank those who allowed me to interview them. They include Ray Crowe, Bill Scott, Marcus Stewart Jr., Bill Hampton, Hallie Bryant, Willie Gardner, Dr. Russell Lane, Willie Merriweather, Bailey Robertson Sr., Bailey Robertson Jr., Angela Jewell, Alonzo Watford, Marie Watford, Tom Sleet, Al Spurlock, Mary Ogelsby, Oscar Robertson, Bob Collins, Garry Donna, Paul D. "Tony" Hinkle, Mayor Alex Clark, Bobby Plump, Gilbert Taylor, Dr. Russell Lane, Betty Crowe, John Grigley, Jerry Oliver, George McGinnis, and Jimmie Angelopolous.

I thank Attucks's principal Lauren Franklin and Patricia Payne, director of the Office of Racial Equality for the Indianapolis Public Schools, for encouragement and assistance. Thanks to Josiah Herndon, a senior at Attucks High when I spoke with him, for sharing the perspective of a contemporary Attucks student. Thanks to Helen Bledsoe for sharing her memory of the post-championship bonfire, and to Bob Wait, a cheerleader swept into a historic event.

I am deeply indebted to scholars and historians Wilma Moore, Emma Lou Thornbrough, Dale Glenn, Dr. Ralph Gray, and Dr. Stanley Warren.

My publisher, Farrar Straus Giroux, an imprint of Macmillan Children's Publishing Group, cared passionately for this story from the beginning. Thanks especially to Joy Peskin, Molly B. Ellis, Morgan Rath, Jeremy Ross, Lucy Del Priore, and John Nora. Particular thanks to copy editor Janet Renard, production editor Nancy Elgin, and designer Monique Sterling. My editor, Wesley Adams, shared fully in the development of this story. I can't thank him enough for a great partnership. And my deep appreciation to editorial assistants Megan Abbate and Melissa Warten, who patiently and diplomatically overcame my IT woes, helped acquire photo permissions, and performed countless other tasks related to this project.

For assistance with the images, thanks to Shannon Williams and Oseye Boyd at *The Indianapolis Recorder*, Becky Marangelli at Ball State University, Patricia Boulos at Boston Atheneum, Sally Childs-Helton at

Butler University, Robert Chester at the Crispus Attucks Museum, Chris May at the Indiana Basketball Hall of Fame, Nadia Kousari at the Indiana Historical Society, Annie Pratt at *USA Today* and Gannett reprints, and John Terhune at *The Washington Times*.

Kirsten Cappy read an early draft and provided invaluable comments. And one of Indiana's most acclaimed authors, Dan Wakefield, met me in a booth at the famed Red Key Tavern and schooled me as only he can about Indianapolis of the 1950s. Thank you, Dan.

Tim Hoose, best of all brothers, helped in every way. My daughters, Hannah Hoose and Ruby Hoose, encouraged me at every turn, and probably learned a bit about the Indiana in which their dad grew up.

And bottomless thanks to Sandi Ste. George, who listened to me read aloud draft after draft, commented on the text, and helped me every step of the way as only she can.

The Times That Followed

Here's what happened later in life to some of the people in this book.

From the 1951 Team

Hallie Bryant: After graduation from Crispus Attucks High in 1953, Hallie was named "Mr. Basketball," the best high school player in Indiana. He played three years for Indiana University, helping the Hoosiers to a share of the Big Ten title in 1957. After a two-year stint in the U.S. Army, Hallie joined the Harlem Globetrotters and remained with the team for twenty-seven years, thirteen as a player. He is a true globetrotter, having visited eighty-seven nations. For many years, Hallie performed a "one-man show" of basketball tricks at the halftime of Globetrotter games.

Coach Ray Crowe: After compiling one of the greatest coaching records in the history of high school basketball in Indiana (179 wins, 20 losses), Coach Crowe retired in 1958, a move he instantly regretted. He then applied for coaching jobs at several schools, including Shortridge High. Everyone turned him down. "For the record he amassed," Oscar Robertson later remarked in disgust, "he should have been coaching at Indiana University." The former coach sold hair products, became an Indiana state legislator, and then served as the director of the Indianapolis Department of Parks and Recreation. He remained close to many of his former players, most of whom continued to call him "Mr. Crowe" until he died in 2003.

Willie Gardner: After several years on the Harlem Globetrotters' traveling team, Willie was signed by the NBA's New York Knicks when he was twenty-three, and immediately bought a house for his mother on the same block as Ray Crowe. But after ten NBA games, a routine physical examination by the Knicks doctor detected a hole in his heart—the doctor called it a "silent heart attack." The Knicks released Gardner, and no other team would take a chance on him. His playing days at an end, he returned to Indianapolis, sold beer for a brewery, and then became a sheriff's deputy. Willie Gardner died in 2000.

Bob Jewell: Dr. Lane's protégé found the adjustment to college rocky at first. He made failing grades at the University of Michigan and then transferred back home to Indiana Central, majoring in chemistry. After graduation, he had trouble finding and keeping a job. In 1956, after being laid off from a construction job, he was referred to a minority employment program run by the American Friends Service Committee— Quakers—and regained his confidence. A letter of reference from Dr. Lane, citing Jewell's Trester Award as evidence of his outstanding character, helped him become the first salaried African American to be hired by the Eli Lilly pharmaceutical company. Jewell steadily worked his way up to a position as a product chemist, where he orchestrated testing of new drugs. Bob Jewell died in 1992.

Bailey "Flap" Robertson: Bailey was named one of Indiana's ten best players in his senior year at Attucks, 1953. He won a basketball scholarship to Indiana Central College, where he was twice named a Small College All-American and became the school's all-time leading scorer, with 2,280 points, averaging more than 24 points per game. He played briefly in the NBA with Cincinnati and Syracuse, and with the Harlem Globetrotters. After a stint in the U.S. Army, Bailey spent much of his career as a special education instructor with the Indianapolis Public Schools system. He died in 1994.

From the 1955 Team

Bill Brown: After being named to the Indiana All-Star team his senior year at Attucks, Bill attended Tennessee State College, where he played on the 1957 basketball team that went on to win the National Association of Intercollegiate Athletics tournament, thus becoming the first all-black collegiate championship team in U.S. history. After playing professional basketball in the Eastern League, Bill became an Indianapolis fireman.

Bill Hampton: Like Bailey Robertson, Bill played at Indiana Central College after graduating from Attucks. He became a high-scoring star, a two-time all-conference selection. After college he played semiprofessional basketball with the Ray Crowe Stars and the Oilers of Holland, Michigan. Bill worked for the Marion County Sheriff's Office as a prison guard, became a manager for an insurance company, and owned his own janitorial service before retiring.

Willie Merriweather: At six-five, Willie was versatile enough to play all positions and became a star at Purdue University. He was named an All-American at guard, averaging 20 points a game. He was selected as an alternate on the 1960 U.S. Olympics team. After his playing days, Willie moved to Detroit and became an outstanding science teacher, quickly working his way through the Detroit school system. He was named Teacher of the Year and served as principal at Denby High School. He also became a player agent for several NBA players, including Hall-of-Famer George Gervin.

Sheddrick Mitchell: Born in Mississippi, the great center on the 1955 team played for Butler University and then was drafted into the U.S. Navy. He later played basketball for Bryant University in Rhode Island, where he received a degree in economics. He lives in Fort Wayne, Indiana.

Oscar Robertson: When Oscar graduated from Attucks in June 1956, he was regarded as the finest high school player in the United States. More than seventy-five colleges recruited him. After visiting Indiana University, where he was insulted by coach Branch McCracken, and the University of Michigan, where no one remembered to meet his plane, he chose the University of Cincinnati. He was the outstanding college player of his era, leading the nation in scoring three years in a row. He co-captained the undefeated, gold-medal-winning 1960 U.S.

men's Olympic basketball team. After fourteen NBA seasons with the Cincinnati Royals and Milwaukee Bucks, he was declared, by Kareem Abdul-Jabbar and others, "the greatest player ever to play the game of basketball." He was the league's most valuable player in 1964 and was inducted into the NBA Hall of Fame in 1980. He played economically, with, as one put it, "the mind of an engineer and the heart of an assassin." In thirty years of competition, Oscar never dunked a basketball in a game. The first player to average a triple-double for an entire season (a double-digit total in three of five possible statistical categories: points, total rebounds, assists, steals, and blocks), he holds the NBA's career record for triple-double games (181) and previously held the single-season record of 41, which Russell Westbrook broke on April 9, 2017.

Oscar was elected the first president of the National Basketball Players Association, where he proved himself, once again, to be a strong and tough leader. *Robertson v. National Basketball Association* of 1970, an antitrust lawsuit, led to changes in the NBA's free agency and draft rules and, in the end, to more freedom and higher salaries for all players. Today Oscar Robertson is a Cincinnati-based businessman who owns several companies.

Bill Scott: Bill played at Franklin College and Butler University, from which he graduated. He then taught at Attucks and became the head boys' basketball coach. He taught, coached, and worked as a counselor for the Indianapolis Public Schools for nearly forty years.

Sources

Author Interviews

Interviews, most of them tape-recorded, were my primary source of information. Between 1986 and 2017, I interviewed more than two dozen players, coaches, cheerleaders, students, historians, politicians, entrepreneurs, and sportswriters. Cassette recordings of the conversations will be archived by the Indiana Historical Society at the conclusion of this project. Interviewees included Jimmie Angelopolous, Hallie Bryant, Alex Clark, Bob Collins, Betty Crowe, Ray Crowe, Basil DeJernett, Willie Gardner, John "Chick" Grigley, Bill Hampton, Tony Hinkle, Bob Jewell, Russell Lane, Graham Martin, George McGinnis, Willie Merriweather, Wilma Moore, Bobby Plump, Bailey Robertson Jr., Bailey Robertson Sr., Oscar Robertson, Bill Scott, Tom Sleet, Al Spurlock, Marcus Stewart Jr., Harold Stolkin, Emma Lou Thornbrough, Stanley Warren, and Alonzo Watford.

Films and Videos

The 1955 and 1956 championship games can be viewed in their entirety on YouTube. Highlights from the 1951 games are also available. The films are worn and ragged after all these years, with patches and holes, but the sound is still consistent, and watching these games gives you a clear sense of Attucks's dominance and excellence.

1951 IHSAA State Semifinal/Championship Highlights. Filmed March 1951. YouTube video (32:24): youtube.com/watch?v=GzsChP0byts. Posted November 2015 by the Indiana High School Athletic Association.

1955 IHSAA State Championship: Indianapolis Crispus Attucks 97, Gary Roosevelt 74. Filmed March 19, 1955. YouTube video (48:34): youtube.com/watch?v=gWgXd7i1iIo. Posted November 2015 by the Indiana High School Athletic Association.

1956 IHSAA State Championship: Indianapolis Crispus Attucks 79, Lafayette Jefferson 57. Filmed March 17, 1956. YouTube video (41:07): youtube.com

/watch?v=hmVakfAJwkM&t=215s. Posted November 2015 by the Indiana High School Athletic Association.

Attucks: The School That Opened a City. Parts 1 and 2. 113-minute documentary. Directed by Ted Green. Indianapolis: WFYI Public Media, 2016; wfyi.org /programs/attucks. Presents Crispus Attucks High's history and social context, stressing the accomplishments of the school's graduates. Features interviews with many of Attucks's notable alumni.

Crispus Attucks Crazy Song. Filmed February 25, 2015. YouTube video (1:15): youtube.com/watch?v=QftykvcKfRY. Posted February 2015 by 19nine. In 2015, Butler University honored the 1955 and 1956 Attucks teams. At the ceremony, several of their original cheerleaders celebrated by singing the "Crazy Song" once again.

Lockefield Gardens: A Community Within a Community. Documentary. Directed by Bradley K. Sims. Indianapolis: Government Cable Channel 16, 1988. This is a brief film about the housing project near Indiana University—Purdue University Indianapolis that brought pride to its residents.

Something to Cheer About. Documentary. Directed by Betsy Blankenbaker. 2002. YouTube video (64:22): youtube.com/watch?v=PscedqISERY. Posted March 15, 2016, by Popcornflix. This 64-minute film about the Crispus Attucks basketball teams of the 1950s includes appearances by Attucks greats Oscar Robertson, Willie Merriweather, Hallie Bryant, and many others.

Books

Angevine, Eric. *Hinkle Fieldhouse: Indiana's Basketball Cathedral.* Charleston, SC: The Hickory Press, 2015.

Chalmers, David M. *Hooded Americanism: The History of the Ku Klux Klan.* New York: Franklin Watts, 1981.

Christgau, John. *The Origins of the Jump Shot: Eight Men Who Shook the World of Basketball.* Lincoln: University of Nebraska Press, 1999.

Glenn, Dale. *The History of the Indiana High School Basketball Association.* Garfield, IN: Mitchell-Fleming Printing, 1976.

Graham, Thomas R., and Rachel Cody Graham. *Getting Open: The Unknown Story of Bill Garrett and the Integration of College Basketball.* Bloomington: Indiana University Press, 2008.

Gray, Ralph D. *Indiana History: A Book of Readings*. Bloomington: Indiana University Press, 1994.

Halberstam, David. *The Breaks of the Game*. New York: Ballantine Books, 1990.

Hamilton, Donald Eugene. *Hoosier Temples: A Pictorial History of Indiana's High School Basketball Gyms*. St. Louis, MO: G. Bradley, 1993.

Hoose, Phillip M. *Hoosiers: The Fabulous Basketball Life of Indiana*, 3rd ed. Bloomington: Indiana University Press, 2016. I included a chapter about Attucks High in this book, first published in 1986 by Vintage Books.

———. *Claudette Colvin: Twice Toward Justice*. New York: Farrar Straus Giroux, 2009.

———. *We Were There, Too! Young People in U.S. History*. New York: Farrar Straus Giroux, 2001.

Leibowitz, Irving. *My Indiana*. Englewood Cliffs, NJ: Prentice Hall, 1964. Leibowitz was a brilliant writer and a fearless, hardworking reporter. His work on the Indiana Klan won the *Indianapolis Times* a Pulitzer Prize.

Lutholtz, M. William. *Grand Dragon: D. C. Stephenson and the Ku Klux Klan*. West Lafayette, IN: Purdue University Press, 1991.

Lynd, Robert S., and Helen Merrell Lynd. *Middletown: A Study in Modern American Culture*. New York: Harcourt Brace Jovanovich, 1956. First published in 1929, the Middletown studies were sociological case studies of Muncie, Indiana, conducted by these husband-and-wife sociologists. There are telling stories throughout the book about the importance of high school basketball.

Marshall, Kerry D. *The Ray Crowe Story: A Legend in High School Basketball*. Indianapolis: High School Basketball Cards of Indiana, 1992. This biography was especially helpful to me in presenting Coach Crowe's boyhood, his high school and college years, and his life before he began to teach and coach at P.S. 17 in 1945.

Raisor, Philip. *Outside Shooter: A Memoir*. Columbia, MO: University of Missouri Press, 2003. Phil Raisor was a starting guard on the Muncie Central teams that lost to Milan in the 1954 state finals and to Attucks the following year. A fine writer, he became a college professor of English.

Reese, William J., ed. *Hoosier Schools: Past and Present*. Bloomington: Indiana University Press, 1998.

Roberts, Randy. *"But They Can't Beat Us": Oscar Robertson and the Crispus Attucks Tigers*. Champaign, IL: Sports Publishing, 1999.

Robertson, Oscar. *The Big O: My Life, My Times, My Game*. Emmaus, PA: Rodale

Press, 2003. Robertson wrote this insightful memoir featuring an extensive section on his boyhood in Tennessee and Indiana, and his years as a player for Crispus Attucks's basketball teams.

Sancton, Tom. *Song for My Fathers: A New Orleans Story in Black and White*. New York: Other Press, 2006. This is the best description and explanation I've ever read of *Plessy v. Ferguson*, the Supreme Court case that legalized racial segregation and ushered in the Jim Crow years—saying it was all right to separate the races as long as they got "equal" treatment.

Schwomeyer, Herbert Frederic. *Hoosier Hysteria: A History of Indiana High School Boys Basketball*, 9th ed. Indianapolis: H. Schwomeyer, 1997.

Thornbrough, Emma Lou. *Since Emancipation: A Short History of Indiana Negroes, 1863–1963*. Indiana Division, American Negro Emancipation Centennial Authority, 1963, 16–23.

Tunis, John R. *Yea! Wildcats!* New York: Harcourt, Brace, 1944. This great fictional account of a small Indiana city swept away by Hoosier Hysteria (sounds like Kokomo to me) contains wonderful descriptions of going to a tourney.

Warren, Stanley. *Crispus Attucks High School: "Hail to the Green, Hail to the Gold."* Virginia Beach, VA: Donning Co., 1998.

———. "The Evolution of Secondary Education for Blacks in Indianapolis." In *Indiana's African-American Heritage: Essays from* Black History News and Notes, ed. Wilma L. Gibbs. Indianapolis: Indiana Historical Society Press, 2007.

Wilkerson, Isabel. *The Warmth of Other Suns: The Epic Story of America's Great Migration*. New York: Random House, 2010.

Newspapers

The many columns and reports that appeared in the Indianapolis newspapers of the day were an invaluable resource. I relied on articles from the daily *Indianapolis Star*, the *Indianapolis News*, the *Indianapolis Times*, and, most revealing of all, the weekly *Indianapolis Recorder*, which was aimed at a black readership. The *Recorder* is included in the following excellent, easily searchable online archive: newspapers.library.in.gov.

During the 1950s, Indianapolis had no major-league sports teams. (The Indiana Pacers were first established in 1967 as a member of the American Basketball Association and became a member of the National Basketball

Association in 1976 as a result of the ABA—NBA merger, and it wasn't until the 1984 season that the National Football League's Colts began playing in Indianapolis.) That, coupled with Indiana's hysteria for high school basketball, caused the city's high school teams to be covered by newspapers as if they were professional teams. Crispus Attucks's ascendancy—and especially Oscar Robertson's heroic talent—was written about almost daily by the city's best reporters.

In preparing to write this book, I was lucky to extensively interview, and befriend, two key newspapermen: Bob Collins, who became the sports editor for the *Indianapolis Star* and died in 1995, and Marcus Stewart Jr., former publisher of the *Indianapolis Recorder*, who died in 2010. Bob and Marcus also helped me access key newspaper archival resources.

Specific articles are cited in the notes.

Magazines and Periodicals

Two periodicals were especially helpful: *Black History News and Notes*, a quarterly publication of the Indiana Historical Society Library, and *Mississippi Valley Historical Review: A Journal of American History*, the official journal of the Mississippi Valley Historical Association.

Goudsouzian, Aram. "'Ba-ad, Ba-a-ad Tigers': Crispus Attucks Basketball and Black Indianapolis in the 1950s." *Indiana Magazine of History* 96, no. 1 (March 2000): 5—43.

Warren, Stanley. "The Other Side of Hoosier Hysteria." *Black History News and Notes* 54 (November 1993): 1—8.

Special Collections

American Negro Emancipation Centennial Authority, Indiana Division collection, Rare Books and Manuscripts, Indiana State Library, pp. 16—23. Indianapolis, 1963.

Russell A. Lane Collection. M522. Indiana Historical Society.

Notes

Introduction: Oscar's Contention

1 Whites could see his talent: Halberstam, *The Breaks of the Game*, 344.

2 the most admired person in Indianapolis: Goudsouzian, "'Ba-ad, Ba-a-ad Tigers,'" 38.

3 "You know," Oscar said: Author interview with Oscar Robertson.

3 "The blanket of fear": See Hoose, *We Were There, Too!*, 213.

4 "Persons unfamiliar with our state may believe": *Indianapolis Recorder*, March 26, 1955.

Prologue: Flap's Shot

The prologue is based on author interviews with Bailey "Flap" Robertson and Oscar Robertson, as well as Stanley Warren, teacher, historian, and a member of the 1951 Attucks team, who watched Flap's shot from the bench.

7 Attucks versus Anderson regional final: *Indianapolis Recorder*, March 10, 1951, and the March 4, 1951, issues of the *Indianapolis Times* and the *Indianapolis Star*.

9 "After Flap's shot": Robertson, *The Big O*, 18.

1. North Toward Hope

This chapter is based on author interviews with Hallie Bryant, Willie Gardner, Willie Merriweather, and Bailey Robertson Jr.

12 Robertson family exodus from Tennessee to Indianapolis: Author interview with Bailey Robertson Jr.; Robertson, *The Big O*, 4—6.

14 The Great Migration (sidebar): Wilkerson, *The Warmth of Other Suns*.

15 Description of Indiana's attitude and behavior toward blacks during migration years: Author interview with historian Emma Lou Thornbrough; Thornbrough, *Since Emancipation*; Warren, "The Evolution of Secondary Education for Blacks in Indianapolis," 7; *Attucks: The School That Opened a City* (film), especially part 1; Gray, *Indiana History*; Roberts, *"But They Can't Beat Us,"* 20—28.

17 D. C. Stephenson and the Ku Klux Klan in Indiana: Lutholtz, *Grand Dragon*; author interview with Emma Lou Thornbrough; Leibowitz, *My Indiana*.

19 "In the rural counties": Leibowitz, *My Indiana*, 217.

22 "a hysteria of belonging": Chalmers, *Hooded Americanism*, 164.

23 turned its attention to public education: Warren, "The Evolution of Secondary Schooling for Blacks in Indianapolis, 1869—1930," 29—34.

26 Crispus Attucks: First to Defy, First to Die (sidebar): See essay "Crispus Attucks" from online collection of resources for the documentary series *Africans in America: America's Journey through Slavery* (produced by WGBH Boston for PBS) at www.pbs.org/wgbh/aia/part2/2p24.html.

27 "Parades of masked Klansmen": Diane Frederick, "Attucks Is Smallest IPS High School," *Indianapolis News*, December 12, 1980.

2. Hoosier Hysteria

31 Big Three visit to Arthur Trester: Warren, "The Other Side of Hoosier Hysteria," 1—8; Glenn, *The History of the Indiana High School Basketball Association*, 120—23.

32 Arthur Trester biography and description: Glenn, *The History of the Indiana High School Basketball Association*, 90, 136—143.

32 What Is a Hoosier? (sidebar): Jeffrey Graf, "The Word 'Hoosier'" (Reference Services Department, Herman B. Wells Library, Indiana University—Bloomington, 2016), https://libraries.indiana.edu/word -hoosier-shorter-version.

33 History of early days of the Indiana High School Basketball Tournament: See Schwomeyer, *Hoosier Hysteria* for a year-by-year essay and box score of each final game starting with 1911; Hoose, *Hoosiers*, 9—33, for a history of the tournament's development; and Tunis, *Yea! Wildcats!*

34 Muncie gym story: Reese, *Hoosier Schools*.

34 Gym Crazy (sidebar): Hamilton, *Hoosier Temples*.

39 Dr. Russell Lane (sidebar): Author interviews with Bob Collins, Betty Crowe, Ray Crowe, and Bob Jewell; Goudsouzian, "'Ba-ad, Ba-a-ad Tigers,'" 9—12; and Russell A. Lane Collection, Indiana Historical Society.

40 Stories of Attucks players and cheerleaders traveling to small towns: Marshall, *The Ray Crowe Story*, 102—04.

41 The Harlem Globetrotters (sidebar): en.wikipedia.org/wiki/Harlem _Globetrotters.

42 Lane's control of player selection, style: Author interviews with Bob Collins, Ray Crowe, and Bob Jewell.

43 IHSAA forced to admit black, Catholic, and private schools: Warren, "The Other Side of Hoosier Hysteria," 5—7.

44 Robertson family living conditions at Frog Island: Robertson, *The Big O*, 7—15.

44 Kinkaid's Hole anecdote: *Attucks: The School That Opened a City* (film), part 2.

46 Lockefield's basketball court: *Lockefield Gardens* (film); Robertson, *The Big O*, 19—24, 43—45.

47 Toughness of play at Lockefield: Author interviews with Hallie Bryant, Bailey Robertson, and Stanley Warren.

48 "I was about seventeen": *Attucks: The School That Opened a City* (film).

48 Oscar Robertson's Christmas basketball: Author interview with Bailey Robertson; also Robertson, *The Big O*, 14.

3. Ray Crowe: "I Would Love to Meet Your Family"

Most of the material in this chapter is derived from lengthy author interviews with Ray Crowe that took place between 1985 and 1995, always in his home office. The taped conversations began as source material for a magazine piece, and then we began to see the story as a possible screenplay. Crowe's office walls were lined with team photos from the great Attucks squads. He frequently consulted a small brown notebook just to make sure he was providing accurate information. A second key source was Kerry D. Marshall's authorized biography, *The Ray Crowe Story*.

52 Big Dave DeJernett (sidebar): Author interview with Dave's brother Basil DeJernett, 1985.

58 P.S. 17 discipline issues, Crowe's after-school program: Author interviews with Hallie Bryant, Willie Gardner, and Bailey Robertson Jr.

60 "[Some houses were] shacks": Marshall, *The Ray Crowe Story*, 53.

4. Gentlemen or Warriors?

63 "The first mighty surge of Ray Crowe's Tigers": "The Indianapolis Tigers," editorial, *Indianapolis Recorder*, March 14, 1953.

64 Attucks under Coach Fitzhugh Lyons, Lyons's departure: Marshall, *The Ray Crowe Story*, 30–32; Roberts, *"But They Can't Beat Us,"* 46–48; author interviews with Bob Collins, Ray Crowe, Bob Jewell, and Bailey Robertson Jr.

64 "One time there was a collision": Author interview with Bob Collins.

64 "I remember one little school": Author interview with Bailey Robertson Jr.

65 Shooting with One Hand (sidebar): Author interview with Hallie Bryant; Christgau, *The Origins of the Jump Shot*.

66 The team he fielded in 1950: Author interviews with Bob Collins, Ray

Crowe, Willie Gardner, and Bob Jewell; Hoose, *Hoosiers*, 65—68; Roberts, *"But They Can't Beat Us,"* 46—49.

67 "I don't know how many times he told me": Author interview with Willie Gardner.

69 Now Frog Island throbbed with excitement: *Indianapolis Recorder*, February 24, 1951.

69 The 1951 Indianapolis regional final: Roberts, *"But They Can't Beat Us,"* 6, 9—13; author interviews with Ray Crowe, Bob Jewell, Bailey Robertson Jr., Oscar Robertson, and Marcus Stewart Jr.

70 "I saw the greatest high school basketball game I've ever seen": Jimmie Angelopolous, *Indianapolis Times*, March 4, 1951.

72 "This might as well be the story of any basketball team": Jimmie Angelopolous, "Attucks Success Story: A Love for Basketball," *Indianapolis Times*, March 11, 1951; author interview with Jimmie Angelopolous.

73 "tidal wave of interracial democracy": "Attucks Tigers and Hoosier Democracy," *Indianapolis Recorder*, March 17, 1951.

73 "The hand of God was on that game": *Indianapolis Recorder*, March 10, 1951.

73 Late in March, the players began to prepare for state finals: Author interviews with Ray Crowe and Willie Gardner.

74 "I couldn't reach his shots": Author interview with Bob Jewell. When I conducted this interview, which took place in the mid-1990s in Indianapolis, I was impressed by Bob's openness, his great self-awareness, and his willingness to discuss the pain that he still felt from the Evansville Reitz loss. He felt that he had let his entire community down, and it hurt that he had never found a way to discuss the loss with his teammates. He carried that hurt after more than forty years. I had the feeling there were no words that would ever remove the sting.

74 Attucks's loss to Evansville Reitz in the final four: For game coverage, see "Upsets Mark Play in Afternoon Tilts," *Indianapolis Times*, March 17, 1951.

For highlights of the game, see *1951 IHSAA State Semifinal/Championship Highlights* (video).

76 the "Crazy Song": *Crispus Attucks Crazy Song* (video).

78 Basketball became his life: Robertson, *The Big O*, 19—22.

78 "It was Oscar": Author interview with Bill Brown.

78 "We'd get out there before everybody": Author interview with Hallie Bryant.

79 "We couldn't go into the south side": Robertson, *The Big O*, 9, 24.

79 "My whole life was Lockefield": Author interview with Bailey Robertson Jr.

80 "He wanted to play bad": *Lockefield Gardens* (film).

81 "I had to run him off the Lockefield court": Ibid.

5. A Form of Jazz   .

84 Discussion of Ray Crowe's control of his players: Author interviews with Ray Crowe, Willie Gardner, Willie Merriweather, Al Spurlock, and Stanley Warren.

86 "It [is] not my job to build basketball teams": Marshall, *The Ray Crowe Story*, preface.

86 "I think a lot of the kids I cut": Ibid., 35.

86 Butler Fieldhouse (sidebar): Author interview with Paul D. "Tony" Hinkle; and Angevine, *Hinkle Fieldhouse*, 12—35.

88 Crowds increased by the game: Hoose, *Hoosiers*, 67—68.

89 Attucks played a form of jazz: Ibid.

91 "[James] Naismith never intended": *Attucks: The School That Opened a City* (film).

91 Attucks Athletic Fund: Author interview with Alonzo Watford.

91 at least toward the athletes who wore green and gold: Author interviews with Willie Merriweather, Bill Scott, and Stanley Warren, among others.

91 "We'd test the places downtown": Author interview with Stanley Warren.

92 "I felt like I'd let my community and school down": Marshall, *The Ray Crowe Story*, 66.

93 Oscar Robertson as a junior high player: Author interviews with Ray Crowe, Willie Merriweather, and Tom Sleet.

6. Ten for the Referees

97 Start of the 1952—53 basketball season, Willie Gardner ineligibility: Author interviews with Ray Crowe and Willie Gardner.

99 "One game with us": My 1985 interview with Alonzo Watford was unforgettable. I met him at his Indianapolis home one evening just a few weeks before he died. Several family members were present. He was stretched flat on a bed and spoke with great difficulty through a plastic oxygen tent. His son, a police officer, had discouraged me from even attempting to speak with him, but his wife, Marie, insisted I try. No one else had ever asked him the questions I had for him that evening. Speech was very difficult for him. Until he thought of those courteous phone calls from athletic directors from other schools—men who but a few months before had refused even to take the court against Attucks—his face had been contorted as he struggled to build words syllable by syllable. But the memories made him chuckle, and soon laughter shook his frame as we spoke.

99 Bernard McPeak story, officiating problems: Author interview with Ray Crowe, corroborated by many players; Marshall, *The Ray Crowe Story*, 91—92. McPeak reapplied in 1954 and was once again rejected. See also "Referees Hold to Jimcrow," *Indianapolis Recorder*, December 4, 1954, and Preston Box, "The Referees Foul Out," *Indianapolis Recorder*, December 11, 1954.

101 The most damaging call of all: Marshall, *The Ray Crowe Story*, 93.

101 "Charles Preston, a writer from the *Indianapolis Recorder*": Author interview with Bob Collins.

105 "Some have called": Charles Preston, "Sportsmen Shocked at 'Fantastic' Call," *Indianapolis Recorder*, March 21, 1953.

105 "I can't think of anything else": "'This Will Be with Me Rest of My Life,' Says Hallie," *Indianapolis Recorder*, March 21, 1953.

105 "After that Shelbyville game": Marshall, *The Ray Crowe Story*, 93.

105 "Many Negro young people": *Indianapolis Recorder*, March 21, 1953.

7. "To Be Around My People"

107 "Eight hours and three hundred miles": Robertson, *The Big O*, 11, 30–31.

108 "For years I had been able to beat him": Author interview with Bailey Robertson.

108 "When I could sense that he could beat me": Author interview with Hallie Bryant.

110 Willie Gardner and Cleve Harp trying out for Globetrotters in Chicago: Author interviews with Ray Crowe and Willie Gardner.

111 "Where'd you find that boy?": Author interview with Willie Gardner.

111 "There were thirty-three rookies": Gregg Doyel, "Willie Gardner Had So Much; Lost So Much," *Indianapolis Star*, June 17, 2016.

112 "I walked home in a daze": Robertson, *The Big O*, 30–31.

113 "Meeting him, seeing him win": Author interview with Willie Merriweather.

114 Bill Scott's family life, living in a garage: Author interview with Bill Scott.

114 got off to a shaky start: Robertson, *The Big O*, 32–33.

115 "poise unexpected of a sophomore": Ibid., 33.

115 "When he got the ball": *Something to Cheer About* (film).

116 "You're Huff": Roberts, *"But They Can't Beat Us,"* 56—58.

117 "If I played, the guy said, he was going to shoot me": Robertson, *The Big O*, pp. 34—35.

117 *Brown v. Board of Education of Topeka* (sidebar): Sancton, *Song for My Fathers*, 186—88.

119 He put Oscar Robertson in the backcourt: Roberts, *"But They Can't Beat Us,"* 59.

119 "Oscar's will was evident": Author interview with Ray Crowe.

120 *Hoosiers*, the Hollywood Film (sidebar): Robertson, *The Big O*, 40—41; Hoose, *Hoosiers*, 47—52.

121 "When we went out to dinner that night": Author interviews with Willie Merriweather and Bobby Plump; Roberts, *"But They Can't Beat Us,"* 62—69.

8. "Attucks Was *Ours*"

126 "Pardon us, fellas": Robert Preston, "And Away We Go!," *Indianapolis Recorder*, October 30, 1954.

126 "I pretty much went through": Robertson, *The Big O*, 46.

127 Crowds increased game by game: "World's Top Crowds Watched Crowemen," *Indianapolis Recorder*, April 2, 1955.

127 "a world's record crowd": Ibid.

129 "When you graduate you pass it on": Author interview with Bill Hampton.

129 "Everywhere I went on the street": Author interview with Bill Scott.

129 "We were special": Author interview with Willie Merriweather.

129 Harold Stolkin, the owner of Indiana Finance: Author interview with Harold Stolkin.

"We have read so much about Oscar": Jimmie Angelopolous, "A Quintet Gets Potshot at Angie," *Indianapolis Times*, January 24, 1956.

131 "Mr. Crowe walked over to Oscar": Author interview with Willie Merriweather.

133 "From now on": Author interviews with Bob Collins, Robert Crowe, and Willie Merriweather, among others; Robertson, *The Big O*, 47.

133 Attucks—Muncie Central showdown: Robertson, *The Big O*, 47–48; Roberts, *"But They Can't Beat Us,"* 98–104.

136 "The week before the finals": Author interview with Russell Lane.

137 "We really didn't know what was going to happen": Author interview with Alex Clark.

138 "What are you doing?": Author interviews with Bill Hampton and Willie Merriweather.

138 "Inspiring even beyond the tournament itself": *Indianapolis Recorder*, March 12, 1955.

139 Bob Wait, Cheerleader (sidebar): Author interview with Bob Wait; "Sportsmanship Forever!," *Indianapolis Recorder*, March 12, 1955. "We have not space to publish all the [cheerleader] names," wrote the editorialist, "but carrot-topped Bob Wait of Broad Ripple high school gets our vote as the city champion in his field of endeavor." And in 2003, Oscar Robertson wrote, "[The intercity] cheer lines . . . touched me back then. Even now it's one of the little details in my life that helps me, when I look back" (*The Big O*, 50).

140 Description of state final game, 1955: Robertson, *The Big O*, 50–51; author interviews with Ray Crowe, Bill Hampton, Willie Merriweather, Oscar Robertson, and Bill Scott; *1955 IHSAA State Championship: Indianapolis Crispus Attucks 97, Gary Roosevelt 74* (video).

140 Post-victory parade: Author interviews with Ray Crowe, Bill Hampton, Bailey Robertson Sr., Oscar Robertson, Bill Scott, Marcus Stewart Jr., and many others. The Attucks victory motorcade has become a hot historical

topic. Oscar Robertson drives the discussion, but he is far from alone. He, and many others, expected that the citywide champs—especially after having won the first championship by an Indianapolis team after forty-four years of trying—deserved and would get a downtown parade, involving grateful fans from all over, probably in daylight hours. But it didn't happen that way. How it did happen is a matter of controversy. Oscar remembers that the motorcade spun around the Monument Circle at the center of the city without stopping and headed straight for Northwestern Park. The *Indianapolis Recorder*, on March 26, 1955, reported it somewhat differently: "About 12,000 persons lined the Monument and wildly cheered as Mayor Clark presented the key to the city to Coach Ray Crowe and the coach in turn introduced his players. Herman Shibler, superintendent of schools, made a brief speech and the team again boarded the fire truck and headed out to Northwestern Park." The *Recorder*'s front page of this issue includes a photo of Ray Crowe accepting the key. But Oscar holds strongly to his memory of the event: "In my recollection we *did not* stop at the circle [Oscar's italics]. The motorcade completed the circle and headed up along Indiana, and then north on West Street" (*The Big O*, 52). In any event, the parade, whose timing—very late on a chilly late-winter night—and whose destination, Northwestern Park, was unknown to most whites, deprived residents of Indianapolis a chance to rejoice as an entire, unified, happy city.

146   "Did they think we'd riot": Robertson, *The Big O*, 53—54.

146   Helen Bledsoe (sidebar): Author interview with Helen Bledsoe.

147   "It didn't bother me": Author interview with Bill Scott.

147   "Relief": Author interview with Ray Crowe.

148   "I kept thinking, 'Attucks means black'": Author interview with Marcus Stewart Jr.

9. Perfection

152   "The boy's daddy walked up to him": *Indianapolis Monthly*, March 2005 (reprinted March 24, 2014, indianapolismonthly.com/news-opinion /remember-the-tigers).

152 "Nobody, I mean nobody, saw the whole court": Roberts, *"But They Can't Beat Us,"* 126.

153 "the greatest scorer in Indianapolis history": Ibid., 135—36.

154 "He hit from under": "Oscar Is Magnificent as He Hits 62 over Spartans," *Indianapolis Recorder*, February 18, 1956.

155 Montgomery, Alabama, bus boycott: See Hoose, *Claudette Colvin*.

155 "The main stories in Montgomery and Indianapolis": Roberts, *"But They Can't Beat Us,"* 145.

159 Oscar injures hand in tournament game: Marshall, *The Ray Crowe Story*, 146—47.

159 Indianapolis officials huddled once again: Author interview with Alex Clark.

161 Attucks versus Lafayette Jefferson for the state title: Marshall, *The Ray Crowe Story*, 149; Robertson, *The Big O*, 56—57; *1956 IHSAA State Championship: Indianapolis Crispus Attucks 79, Lafayette Jefferson 57* (video).

165 "That Oscar Robertson is the greatest": Roberts, *"But They Can't Beat Us,"* 162.

167 1956 victory parade: Robertson, *The Big O*, 58.

167 Oscar did something impulsive: Roberts, *"But They Can't Beat Us,"* 165.

10. Legacy

170 "Break up the Attucks dynasty!": Author interview with Ray Crowe.

170 "The success of Attucks's basketball": Author interview with Bob Collins.

170 "We gave the black community hope": *Indianapolis Monthly*, March 2005 (reprinted March 24, 2014, indianapolismonthly.com/news-opinion /remember-the-tigers).

170 "I don't think it had ever happened before": Ibid.

171 "The N-word was used": Author interview with a woman who asked that her name not be identified.

171 "He was like our Rosa Parks": Ray Tolbert in Jeff Rabjohns, "Robertson Became 'Big O' During Endless Hours Perfecting Game on Indy Playground," the bigo.com/AboutOscarRobertson/IndyPlayground.php.

171 "[Oscar] was our prince": Author interview with George McGinnis.

171 Breakup of the Frog Island neighborhood, impact of Attucks's racial integration: *Attucks: The School That Opened a City*, especially part 2; *Lockefield Gardens* (film); author interviews with Wilma Moore (senior archivist of African American history at the Indiana Historical Society) and Stanley Warren.

172 "It's the only time I ever saw my dad cry": Author interview with Patricia Payne.

172 "Many of my fondest memories": Marshall, *The Ray Crowe Story*, 167.

173 Crispus Attucks High School today: Author conversation with Attucks's current principal, Lauren Franklin, along with a school visit and a tour of the facility. See also "Retro Indy: Crispus Attucks High School, *Indianapolis Star*, February 24, 2014, indystar.com/story/news/history/retroindy/2014/02/24/crispus-attucks/5774495.

173 Josiah Herndon, Attucks Class of 2017 (sidebar): Author interview with Josiah Herndon.

176 Attucks's 3-A 2017 high school championship: For game coverage, including highlight reel and video of Oscar Robertson's response at the buzzer, see Kyle Neddenriep, "Crispus Attucks' State Title Is 'Bigger Than Basketball,'" *Indianapolis Star*, March 26, 2017, indystar.com/story/sports/high-school/2017/03/25/crispus-attucks-wins-first-state-title-since-1959/99380574.

177 The Parade That Wasn't (sidebar): *Indianapolis Star*, May 23, 1955.

Index